Who's Driving Your Bus?

A simple solution to the complex challenge of managing your emotions.

Kim Johnson

Best-selling author · Master Mindset Coach · Creative Strategist

Forward by Cami Bass

The author of this book does not dispense medical advice or prescribe the use of any technique as a form of treatment for physical, emotional, or medical problems without the advice of a physician, either directly or indirectly. The intent of the author is only to offer information of a general nature to help you in your journey for emotional, physical, and spiritual well-being. In the event you use any of the information in this book for yourself, the author, and publisher assume no responsibility for your actions.

First edition, August, 2019

ISBN: 978-0-578-57236-9

Thoughts directly from Kim's One-on-One Clients...

"I started coaching just over two years ago with Kim. I had never been a fan of phone coaching but after our first session I knew we would work well together. Kim has given me tools, protocols and advice to grow my practice. In fact we have grown over 300% in two years. I would highly recommend Kim if your goal is to improve your business and free yourself from all the traps that we can get stuck in through the process. Kim has also be instrumental in helping me achieve clarity of who and what I expect to have in my life. Thank you Kim Johnson for being there for me always!!" - *Dr. Ransom M.*

"Kim is the best thing thats ever happened to me! Kim showed me that anything I want is possible & I had my own business just 6 months later! She has always been supportive and most of all patient. Not a phone call wasted in 2 yrs. Kim has always given me her full attention and respect. She would do anything for her clients, and thats just rare!! She guided me through every obstacle in my way. Im absolutely grateful and blessed to have Kim in my life!" - *Joyce A.*

"I started as one of Kim's Coaching clients and I was looking for coaching on a more personal (life coaching) capacity and soon discovered her talents for business coaching as well. Kim is caring and honest and she is very creative. Within a few weeks of starting my coaching program I saw huge benefits in connecting with Kim. She's a keen listener and comes up with creative tips and techniques to tackle challenges. She is direct and sincere and I love that she is able to tell it like it is, which is something I looked for in a coach. Thanks to Kim I have grown tremendously as a person and in my business. She is also funny and super easy to work with. I highly recommend her to anyone that is committed to making a change in their life." - *Nilu K.*

"As a performing artist, I assumed that my first session with a life coach would be about all the stuff I had been straining myself to learn. Organization, money, follow-through, etc To my delight, her first advice was to make more time for creativity. My brain said, "WHAT?! That can't be right." It was clear in my 6 months with Kim that her endgame was about my happiness and satisfaction in life all the time, not just "fixing" my flaws. In the end, I did learn some advanced organizational skills and even utilize a good chunk of them daily. I am grateful for the level of personal understanding and connection Kim was willing to give. Also, let's not forget about the undying patience that was required of her to work with a woman who, wait for it, couldn't even figure out how to use a pencil without breaking it, at first. That's how challenged I was at keeping a calendar. I could not operate the pencil. Sheesh. Kim is smart, well-trained, intuitive and invested and she is not shy about sharing all of it to help create a better, happier world, one pencil-failing soul at a time."
- *Bronwen B.*

"Kim is infectiously upbeat and understands, better than most, how to navigate through a tedious world toward knowing and fulfilling one's ultimate purpose. Her presence at a gathering is palpable; her energy fuels those in her sphere. Kim uniquely exudes a refreshingly secure sense of self-assuredness without an ounce of off-putting egotism. This combination allows her to effectively penetrate the psyches of her clients and nurture their senses of personal awareness from the inside out. Working with Kim will put you on a rapid pathway toward your own possibilities." - *Ron B.*

"Coaching with Kim was one of the best decision in my life. She make me realize that there is so many things that I can accomplish in life, she is very talented and creative in so many ways. Pushing me to achieve and accomplish my goal and my dream, so we can live a fulfilled life. I raise my hat to her!!"
- *Rachael H.*

"Kim is a master strategizer for any sort of situation. Whether the issue relates to business, health, or personal development, she has the ability to help you zero in on the essential information and stop getting stuck in the extraneous details of the problem. She's brilliant!!" - *Anny S.*

"Kim has helped me get focused. I'm further along in just a few weeks then I was trying to work without a coach. She's a tough cookie and a great coach." - *Liz K.*

"For many years I have been wanting to pull all my life's experiences together and create a business/passion. Like so many of us, I couldn't get out of my own way. Kim changed all of that for me.Working with Kim helped me to clear all the "noise" out of my life. I was missing so many great opportunities while chasing ones that didn't serve me. Kim has an amazing ability to quickly look at what is showing up in your life, what is not, and set you on a path for success. Kim comes to the relationship with so much experience and life skills, that it is hard to believe there is a situation she hasn't tackled. One of Kim's greatest traits is that she sees things to the end. Your goal becomes her goal, and she doesn't quit until you both get to the finish line. My finish line was opening up an Ultra Premium Olive Oil and Balsamic Vinegar store, and on November 1, 2014, I did just that! DASH Oil and Spice Emporium has been a great success and I owe it all to Kim. I don't know where I'd be right now without Kim and her vision. She has become more than just my coach, she has become my friend, and for that I can't thank her enough!" - *Michelle R.*

"I have been coached by Kim for more than 5 years.. from when I felt lost, trapped in my own chain of rules and stuck in life.. but I was certain that I had a profound desire to change my life. I found in Kim not just a professional coach but a trustful soul who from a place of compassion started giving me the structure I wanted to set myself free of judgement and criticism and start creating the life I longed for so long. She became my mentor in authoring and publishing my first book and I still receive guidance from her on setting my own business as well of discovering amazing opportunities that sometimes I don't see clearly. When we finish every session I had a feeling I dream my own clients had... the feeling of unstoppable and believing that it is possible and I can do it. Minds and heart working together. I cannot be more grateful." - *Ismenia A.*

"Quite simply working with Kim has changed the trajectory of my life. Before we started working together I was in a very, very, very low place in my life and I had literally no idea of how to navigate my way out of the situation I was in. Kim's support, insights, patience and compassion have bit by bit enabled me to turn my life around. A year and a half since we began, I am in a loving relationship, I have a strong social network of support around me. I don't have big enough words to say how grateful I am for her help." - *Lara C.*

"I have been working with Kim Johnson for the past five years and I can honestly say that she has been instrumental in truly helping me to take my life to levels that I never really believed possible. On a personal level, after the death of my father, she gave me new perspective and amazing mind-shifts that allowed me to move forward to live in peace and gratefulness. In my career, Ms, Johnson's incredible gifts of strategic and insightful understanding and direction of what it takes to make goals a reality...are priceless! Although theory in any business is important, Ms, Johnson has devised real life tools with actual, workable and clear-cut concepts and plans of action; such as the perfect week, personal beliefs about myself and how they relate to success in my career, and core elements; to name a few. Her experience, knowledge and keen awareness of what is needed to shift your beliefs in an instant is remarkable. Since I began working with Ms. Johnson, I am working on writing my first screen play (which I thought was only a dream), I have developed and outlined a new television show, and my income has doubled!

She is such an integral part of my business plan and personal success that I now consider her a necessary member of my team. Simply put, I believe the most successful and most fulfilled people understand that to be their best, you need to work with the best. Kim Johnson is the key to both my personal and professional success and I recommended her highly. I absolutely would not be where I am in my life and my career today without Ms. Johnson! - *Julia W.*

"I have used Kim personally and professionally for 3+ years with great results.

Personally, she has helped me and my family navigate the loss of our oldest son. Her insight on this matter were life changing and my wife and 2 younger sons will be forever grateful for how she coached me through this transition.

Professionally, she has helped me navigate multiple issues relative to HR and Organizational Development. Most recently I asked Kim to work with our colleagues to help understand the social-emotional dynamics in our business that seemed to be preventing us from being our best selves. Through her interview process, we learned about workload problems, broken processes, mis-aligned organization structure, poor communication habits, poor interpersonal communications and much more. As a result of what we learned, we have re-structured our leadership team, promoted a number of individuals, more actively coached other colleagues and made process changes in support of a more efficient workplace.

Our colleagues had one complaint.....they wanted her to stay longer!!!! They loved her non-judgmental listening skills and trusted her implicitly to carry their concerns back to me....which she did. She helped my see some blind spots in my leadership and our company is stronger as a result.

5 star recommendation." - *Scott G.*

To my husband, Mark.
Without your patience, care and willingness to help me endlessly, I could not have created this book.
I love you beyond words.

Welcome to 'Who's Driving Your Bus?'!

Thank you for joining me on the wonderful ride of emotional intelligence!

If you have found this book first, you may not have seen the video for the The Who's Driving Your Bus 72 Hour Challenge. This video gives you the parameters around the challenge. http://www.authorkimjohnson.com/72hourchallenge

If you found the video first, welcome to the book! The book gives you all the background, concepts and story of Lily & Liz, the ladies who we join during three days of their lives.

Whatever brought you here, thank you. I appreciate you taking the time to join me on this journey. I know that you have many options of where to spend your time and I appreciate your time and faith in this book. Thank you.

Now, Let the ride begin!

Kim

Foreword by Cami Bass

It had taken every ounce of courage I could muster up to make that first phone call to Kim. I had blown her off for two months now, so I took a deep breath, and finally dialed the number. My anxiety must have been apparent, because our conversation was supposed to be going somewhere else when she stopped and asked, "Who's driving your bus right now?"

My bus? What a strange question to ask someone who did not own a bus. I knew I should not have picked up that phone. I hated calling people. I just knew this conversation would be no different than all the others. A disaster. A waste of my time. Anything but good. I definitely knew she was going to be way too positive and perky for me. I sat in on conference calls with Kim, and I had no desire to be on this phone with this person right now. That is how I always thought back then. One of my bus drivers is Negativity. If there was a way to make the situation negative, I could do it. I could sit and complain for hours.

As it turns out, our phone call that day would be a huge turning point in my life, one I don't think I could have ever prepared for. I remember filling up quite a few pages in a journal, jotting down notes. I was trying to preserve everything she was telling me. People have always told me that I can choose happiness, or that I can decide what kind of day I'm going to have, but no one had ever explained to me that in my head, I had different people driving a bus. A bus where each driver who takes the wheel also takes control of my emotional wellbeing. For however long they are steering, that tiny persona has control of my day's destination. It was like my first 'Ah-ha' moment. Before this, never for a second did I believe I had any kind of power over what kind of day, or life, I was going to have. It was all just a bunch of mumbo jumbo to me, but this just made sense.

Before I knew who was driving my bus I was struggling to do everyday things. I had been to several doctors and been diagnosed with different labels along the way. I tried many different medications and I was on a downward spiral that seemed endless. I could barely walk through a grocery store anymore without issue. People were so intimidating for me at that point that if someone looked at me I nearly fell to the ground in the fetal position. Driving was becoming unbearable from the anxiety. Calling people was excruciating. Even showering some days was a fight with myself.

However, now, every day, throughout the day I will find myself asking, "Ok Cami, who is driving your

bus right now?" I'll follow this by quickly deciding who I want to be doing the driving. That can be tricky! Some days I need to be focused, but I also want to be silly. If you know me at all, even during those times that I was struggling so hard, I was often silly. Laughter is one of my favorite things in life. My favorite by-product from this whole bus thing is that I find myself laughing more than I used to. It isn't forced anymore. People, instead of making me want to drop to the ground in fear, make me laugh once again. I speak of switching drivers a lot.
I've said to a few friends with whom I've shared the bus analogy, that by learning about my bus I feel as if my tires were also given new air and I can roll with life again. I'm able to keep moving, like I have a full tank of gas. I feel like I have become the bus. If I just take care of myself... There will be no stopping me.

I will sometimes be caught telling people I need a moment to 'pull my bus over'. I don't think most people get it, but it's just my way of saying I need a few minutes to collect my thoughts, regroup, consciously choose my emotional reality, the one that will best serve me in this moment, and get going again. I think we all need to know how to do that. It's been a lifesaver for me.

Kim's metaphor, along with her continued friendship and support, has changed my life in so many ways I never thought possible! Kim is always one of my first phone calls when something great happens in my life. She was the first person I called when I was offered a new job. Because I am able to work full time now, I can call people or pay my own bills without having panic attacks. I talk to people on the phone, a lot. When entering a store or talking to the cashier I don't even think about it anymore. I just talk to everybody, perhaps too much. I spend a lot more time enjoying things than I do worrying about them. At least I try to. However, when feel I can't, I now know how to switch drivers.

I hope that after reading this book you can identify who is driving your bus, and that you too can switch drivers as many times as necessary to get you to your destination, wherever that may be in life.

All my love,
Cami Bass

The Story of the Bus.

"Sometimes you have to take drastic measures to help yourself" - I can still hear myself saying that to my mother.

There was a time in my life that it seemed I had everything and then some. Everyone around me was telling me that I should be happy. I should be satisfied. I should be content. But I wasn't. I just wasn't. I was everything BUT those things. So I took matters into my own hands and dove head first into self-development. I was completely resolute to grow and make myself a better person, a better teacher, even a better parent. My entire identity centered around changing and shifting the very core of myself. Nothing was going to stop me.

Of course an endeavor like this can be very expensive. I was going to seminars, reading every book I could get my hands on and watching every video I could find.

I begin to notice that as much as I was changing, I felt that there were many concepts that were not sticking. It really began to aggravate me that I was investing so much time and money into transformation, yet I was struggling with the process.

All one must do is open up any random self-development book and start reading. They're often complex with many steps to success which make you want to give up before you start. I was convinced there had to be strategies to simplify this process.

I am very visual. I paint pictures in my mind. Much of what I was learning was more digital and theoretical. It was very hard to paint pictures with this content and even harder to use it in 'the moment'. You know, those moments when you really should be able to manage yourself and yet you can't.

It was really baffling to me that I was investing so much time, money and effort in learning, yet a lot of the learning did not seem to be practical. As soon as something would go wrong in my life, I would often forget everything that I had learned. In those very real moments, I felt ill prepared. The only solution I could come up with at the time was to keep going, satiating myself in the content. I felt like if I could drown out the voice in my head, then maybe I would have a chance. So that's exactly what I did. I decided to make evolving my life my mission. I was going to create the life I wanted no matter what!

Fast forward twenty-two years later, hundreds of books, along with months and months of live seminars and studying, and my life is completely different. When anyone asks me if all of the learning, struggles, money spent and time invested was worth it, I would say, “Yes, without question.” and as a result, something interesting happened along the way; I became a mindset coach. I had always wanted to be a schoolteacher and I was discouraged from doing it as a child.

My father loved me dearly and said to me that although teaching was noble, there wasn’t any money in it. He wanted me to do something so that I made enough money that I could take care of myself. I completely appreciated this and of course, because I adored my father, I listened to him. However that doesn't mean the desire to teach ever went away.

It made perfect sense to me that as a coach, I could teach! So I began writing books. I started out with children's books and then I moved on to productivity books, but the one thing that kept bugging me all along was how to help people make changes in the moment. There had to be a better way.

I kept experimenting with my private clients. I would try stories, analogies and personal challenges like my 90 day challenge. While all of these worked to some degree, there was often a lack of consistency. The clients outcomes were met to their expectations, but in my eyes I knew they could be better. I also knew for myself that I could grow further. I knew in my personal world that I could be a better partner to my husband, a better mother to my children, and a better business person if I could manage my state with ease and grace.

I began this journey with myself first. As a visual person, I had to figure out a way to take this data that was described in very digital ways and convert it into something I could understand and work with immediately.

While all of this was happening in my work world, I still had a family. My son was very young at the time and I was working a lot. The combination of a young child and lots of work doesn't make for great parenting. I was doing the best I could at the time and I thought that I was connecting with him in a pretty great way. Until that edifying moment one afternoon when he was trying to tell me something and I wasn't paying attention. I was responding but I was not focused on him. My mind was somewhere else... and he knew it.

I was sitting on the floor in my office sorting out paperwork. He was standing beside me. As he was telling me his story, I was giving blank answers then he decided to do something that changed my life. He grabbed my face and turned my head towards his. His little fingers, at five years old, turned my head quickly, and he looked directly into my eyes, and said, "Mommy look at me. I'm trying to tell you something important!"

What just happened? I was dumbfounded. In that moment my world changed. I recognized that I was not being the parent I thought I was. Let's face it, we've all been there. If you have children, we've all done this. It is a never ending struggle to balance the worlds we create, but in this moment, I knew I was wrong. I could see the look in his eyes. His mother was not paying attention to him and it broke my heart. That was it for me. I was going to fix this no matter what.

So I decided this would not happen again. I was determined to create a visual way that would help me recognize what was going on mentally, which would allow me to exercise influence over my external world. Over time, I started to think of my thoughts and feelings as a cast of characters. This cast of characters which were metaphorically living inside of me, took on their own personas as I gave them identities and names. As I looked deeper, I began to really know them. I soon came to realize that these characters were really my emotions and feelings, they were a multitude of states that lived within me and ultimately controlled everything in my world. The real question I came to realize was, "Were they controlling me or was I controlling them?"

I later started to think as if these characters were on a bus. Whomever was driving the bus dictated my experience. In that moment, I had a breakthrough. Not a minor breakthrough... a significant breakthrough! Simply asking myself, "Who is driving this bus right now?" changed my immediate focus and allowed me to be in charge of my emotions, regardless of their consequence or tenure. Month after month, day after day, moment after moment, I began to become aware of my cast of characters. Who were my primary bus drivers? Who were the entities that liked to be in cahoots and use their powers for evil? I was akin to a detective on a case, deciphering a mysterious code to unlock the part of myself that was being held hostage by my emotions.

Over the course of the next year, I really began to develop my "bus" concept. I have to admit that it was quite an experience for me. I finally had a decent handle on myself. I could control my reactions about 80% of the time. I was developing the skill to switch gears rapidly, switching from one emotion to another. I was quite mesmerized by it. After all the years of in depth studying along with all that extensive training, I had not experienced something that worked quite so easily and quickly.

I began teaching this to my clients. The results were astounding. They were getting similar results as I had experienced. They had previously not been able to shift their state, but they were readily doing it now. Their level of awareness was increasing. Their level of happiness was growing. Their level of success was rising. Most importantly, they were able to make the strategy work in the moment.

"Who's Driving your Bus?" was born.

I could not have been happier. I was seeing the progress I had always wanted to see in my clients. As luck would have it, one afternoon I was introduced to a very special person. I say introduced but this was over social media. I had been leading a training for a network marketing company, and one of the reps, Cami, sent me a message. After a few conversations with her, I realized how impactful implementing the concept of "Who's Driving your Bus?" was for her. Her confidence was growing everyday.

This interaction with my now friend, Cami, is the reason you're reading this book. Up until this point I didn't think this notion of the bus could have value outside of a long-term coaching client. I knew how helpful it was to me as well as my coaching clients, but I thought I would always need to do the work with them.

Luckily Cami changed everything. Because of her, I recognized that this could benefit others immediately, whether they were involved in coaching or not. I am grateful for all that Cami has taught me about how to bring this forward to all of you. The strategies and lessons you are going to learn about have helped countless clients, Cami and me. My hope is that you find this concept useful in your own life and are able to take command of your emotions.

So let's get started!

The topic of emotions vs feelings has long been debated and blended together. Most of us blend emotions and feelings regularly, making them indistinguishable.

For the purpose of Who's Driving Your Bus, we will be focused on the fact that emotions create feelings and feelings create actions.

This methodology is a coaching approach. Coaching is based on the current place you are and moving forward. Coaching does not look backward since we cannot change the past. If you are looking for methodology to look to the past, please seek a certified therapist.

Emotions can be a very tricky aspect of ourselves to understand. We all have them and we all have to deal with them. Some of us seem to deal with them better than others. Some of us struggle to understand our emotions while others seem to manage them effortlessly. To add fuel to the emotional fire, ***when emotions go up, intelligence goes down.*** Yes, you read that correctly. That works for what you may view as positive emotions as well as what you may call negative emotions. I know for sure that I have made some choices in a peak emotional state, believing I was joyful in that moment, only to come to the conclusion a day later it would have been better to go in a different direction.

Like most of us, my emotions are a huge part of who I am. Some days I feel like a surfer, constantly riding the waves up and down, moment to moment. Other days are like an effortless day at the beach.

In order to begin the journey into this part of awareness, we need to understand that we are intrinsically made up of a seemingly endless number of emotions. What complicates this even more is the fact that while each of us experiences the same emotions, these emotions show up differently within each of us. We all define them differently. Think of it like this: if I ask you to think of the color blue, you envision the color blue. The challenge we have is that your blue and my blue will inevitably be different hues of blue. While we will agree that we both have chosen a blue, they will be different. Those small nuances make all the difference. In the world of emotions, those small nuances are the difference between happiness and sadness for many of us. Being able to understand your personal definitions for each emotion gives you the power to command those emotions. Considering how many emotions we can experience as a human being, coupled with the nuances of those emotions, we have our work cut out for us.

To make matters even trickier, **most of the emotions we experience are not emotions that we consciously chose**. Stop and pause and think about that statement for a moment. As infants, we were far too young to choose our emotions. We were little sponges absorbing what was happening around us. If you grew up with someone who nurtured you with patience, kindness and love, you no doubt have a definition of patience, kindness and love very similar to that person. If you grew up with someone who was nervous and uncertain, or angry and distant, you no doubt have an experience of that emotion within you. So as adults, we are dealing with emotions that we most likely did not consciously choose. I don't know about you, but this frightened me when I'd had this revelation. The last thing I want is some of my un-resourceful relatives taking up space in my head!

Can you see how important this is? You are being driven by emotions that you may or may not have chosen or understand.

Here's another very important fact to remember about emotions; they are here to help us. Our emotions are not here to make us suffer. Our emotions are here to guide us. In the words of one of my favorite mentors and speakers, *Esther Hicks*, "Our emotions are our guidance system." I remember when I heard that from her. It was the first time in all the studying I had done that I had heard it described that way. Esther describes it as a GPS system for human beings... Simply brilliant!

To understand ourselves even further, we must fully dive into emotions.

Emotions are not good or bad. Emotions are not right or wrong. **Emotions are simply the clues to your inner world.** They do, however, hold the key to your well-being.

As emotional creatures, we can't get away from them. They go wherever we go. So picture this... All of your emotions are on a bus inside your head. Your bus, whatever size your bus may be, single level or double-decker, whatever color your bus may be, is filled with a myriad of emotions. Each one of these emotions has its own personality. It has its own rules. It has its own dialogue and language. Interestingly enough, many of these emotions like to work together. Often my clients will ask me if it's possible to experience more than one emotion at a time. My answer is a resounding... YES! Imagine your emotions sitting with each other on the bus.

The bus is filled with this cast of characters. These emotions can even make up their own personas. One of my favorite personas that I have consciously created for myself is my Hippie Chick Zen Girl. I love her because she doesn't get stressed out. She's relaxed and she trusts that things are going to be okay. She's not uptight when the house is messy or we are out of supplies. She simply takes a deep breath and says, “It's all going to be okay.” She is made up of patience, awareness, kindness and love. Her favorite response is “It’s all good.” She is just chilled out.

Now while we have a bus filled with these characters, it’s important to remember that one of these characters, or emotions, is always driving. Whether it's a single emotion or an amalgam of a few, someone is always driving your bus. The driver dictates your experience. Again, stop and pause and think about this. This is a very important distinction. Whatever emotion you are in or whatever persona you have in the driver’s seat, that emotion or persona completely and totally dictates your experience. Emotions can switch seats and change drivers in a heartbeat. In your average day, you can have a surprising number of drivers. Sometimes drivers are there for five minutes and sometimes they're grinding it out all day. The only way you can start to identify the dynamic, is to be observant of what's going on. Awareness and being in the moment is what matters.

To complicate matters even more, we typically have a primary driver. They're not someone that we hired for the job, but someone that by our habitually allowing them to take over, has become a primary driver. For most of us, this is not an emotion that we consciously chose.

Typically, we have three to five favorite drivers that we default to regularly. This happens. Whether we like it or not, they are calling the shots, but that can change.

When I started to explore this for myself, I immediately realized that one of my primary drivers was Certainty. In fact, she is my default driver, the one that shows up automatically when I'm not paying attention. The emotion of Certainty has been hardwired into me. I need to know things ahead of time...WAY AHEAD of time. I want to make sure all of my bases are covered. I will double check things, then triple check things. I want to know what we are doing this Friday night on Monday morning. I want the dishwasher loaded the "right" way. Everything must be in its place. Certainty Girl, as I affectionately call her, has rules for nearly everything and those rules are expected to be followed by everyone. While this is a very effective trait and emotion for some aspects of business and life, this is not an effective trait or emotion for relationships. This drives my husband insane! My need to be at the airport two hours before the flight takes off annoys him. My need for an overstocked pantry leaves him in a state of wonder. My constant and never-ending questions make him stare at me with a blank face wondering, "Why is she asking me this again?". I recognize that Certainty Girl has been with me my entire life.

I'm fairly certain I know when she took the wheel, although I know she has been with me as far back as I can remember, I also know I learned it from my mother. A worrywart to her core, her emotion went beyond certainty and crossed over to worry. As a small child, I witnessed it over and over, and I recognize that I assumed that emotion as my own.

Admittedly, I do like Certainty Girl. She gives me a great sense of comfort that all the details are covered, making me feel in control of my world. In reality, though, she's not great as a long-term driver. She drives everybody else insane!

The trouble for me is that she is the primary driver unless I conscientiously move her out of the driver seat. She will hijack my bus at every opportunity that she gets. And when she gets into the driver's seat, she makes sure she's strapped in with a three-point safety belt, holding onto the steering wheel with white knuckles! She doesn't like to give up driving, and I know it.

She is ever vigilant to the details of my life. She pursues Certainty like a heat-seeking missile. I must attempt to remain in a constant state of awareness to make sure I choose her when I need her, not just accepting her all the time. Can you see yourself in this description? Is Certainty Girl on your bus too?

Another one of my five primary drivers is Creative Girl. She is so dynamic and ALWAYS creating something. She loves to photograph anything and 'sees' pictures constantly. She paints, writes books, gardens...really just about anything she thinks she can make unique, she loves. While all of this sounds so wonderful, just like almost every other emotion, she can have a dark side. If she is sitting next to Certainty Girl or Anxiety Girl, she paints vivid pictures of things going wrong. Those vivid pictures can cause me to hold back, feeling too anxious to move forward. Can you imagine the power they hold?

My three other primary drivers are Curiosity Girl, Anxiety Girl and Gratitude Girl. What a motley crew! As odd as this mix is, they are my crew. They are the primary emotions that drive my bus, and as a result, my life. While there are endless shades of other emotions, these are my core crew.

Curiosity Girl has been with me FOREVER. I love questions, asking questions, studying questions... they all thrill me. Learning is sustained for me by asking questions.

In fact, I asked so many questions as a child that my teacher for sixth, seventh and eighth grade English made me sit facing the wall in the back corner of his classroom as an attempt to break me. It didn't work. Not even one bit.

Curiosity Girl remained with me, thank goodness. You see, she drives all my coaching, creative and strategic business. She always looks for more clues. She is committed to the outcomes of my clients.

Understanding your cast of characters, the emotions they represent and the way they show up should be taught in school. I have yet to find something that helps me as quickly as this. If I simply ask myself the question, "Who is driving my bus right now?" I instantaneously know. I know all of the characteristics of this emotional persona. I know what they're doing for me and they know what they are trying to gain.

Remember, emotions can also sit side by side, amplifying the attributes of each other. Imagine Angry sitting next to Fear. Or Happy next to Anxiety. Knowing who likes to team up will also help you understand what is going on in the moment.

To give you an idea of how my clients describe this concept, here is an excerpt from a client email. As you can see, this client was experiencing multiple emotions and was still able to work through what was going on by simply identifying the emotions involved. She was able to understand how they slipped into the driver seat. If she didn't choose them intentionally, she simply made a mindful choice in that moment and switched them out.

"Hurt, Bitter, and Rage were fighting over the wheel, and then Calm took it away from them. Bewildered has stopped crying and is sniffling in her seat, Determined is trying to comfort me. In a little while Determined will take the wheel and will try to figure out a way to get through the next few weeks without letting myself be manipulated again. Resigned has decided that after the event I will no longer try to have a relationship with this person. We will go back to seeing each other only when necessary and we will be cordial. Part of me is sad for the loss of a friend, but Realistic understands you can't lose something you never had. Now, Determined is going to make sure I get a good night's sleep, and in the morning I will come up with a strategy for dealing with the office stuff."

Over the coming months, this client was well prepared due to feeling fueled by Awareness and Determination driving her bus. She navigated a very emotional time in her life and came out Calm and feeling like she was in control of her situation.

To simplify the process, the 'In-The-Moment Strategy' looks like this:

You feel your emotions going up. You immediately...

***!. STOP** - Actually tell yourself to stop.*

***2. REFLECT** - Breathe. get back into the current moment. Heighten your awareness - "Who is the current driver?"*

***3. CHOOSE** - Ask yourself "Who is a better driver right now ?" Be mindful of your desired outcome.*

***4. REDIRECT** - Once you have awareness, choose a different driver if need be.*

The wonderful thing about all of this is that when you have an awareness of what's going on with your emotions, you can manage and guide them. While it's a simple process, it's not always easy. But knowing that this is possible makes all the difference. It sets you up for success when you are cognizant and aware while driving your bus.

The truth is that in life, we only have control over our emotions, our beliefs, our values, our behaviors and our identity. More concisely put, our interpretations, what things mean to us. When we live in a state of awareness, we can design, create and manage our internal world. When you consistently choose who is driving your bus, you are in control.

Once you are in control, you can make better choices. Better choices lead to better conditions in your life. The formula is most effective when you are consistent.

The secret sauce is made up of awareness, choice, action, and consistency.

As you learn, you burn new pathways and create new patterns from which to operate. When you gain awareness about your emotions and your triggers; and their hold on you, you then have the opportunity to choose something different. When you interrupt the hold that they have on you and choose another emotion, you burn new and improved patterns into your emotional hardwiring. As you make and exercise these changes consistently, real and lasting change is set in motion.

So who are the emotions on your bus?

Have you started thinking about who your primary driver is?

Have you started thinking about the different emotions that drive your bus during a day?

What will you name your drivers?

What can you learn about your drivers? What triggers them to show up?

Who are your top 3 - 5 primary drivers?

Who will your favorite CHOSEN driver be?

Do you have a double-decker bus filled to the brim or a very small bus?

I myself have a double-decker bus that is overfilled with people hanging out the windows!

Have you taken the 72-hour challenge yet? Here is the link authorkimjohnson.com/72hourchallenge to meet me on video and learn about the 72-hour challenge. If you would prefer to read about the challenge, it is outlined at the very back of the book.

I have also included an extensive list of emotions at the end of the book. My suggestion: Visit that section when you finish the book and highlight the ones that resonate with you. Don't judge yourself for having too few or too many.

Whatever your list or level of awareness of your emotions, it's all meant to be just as it is. NO JUDGEMENT driving your bus!

Since we learn best when we can associate through stories, we are about to enter the world of Lily & Liz. Lily is about to take the 72-hour challenge. My hope is that by reading about these two ladies and their lives, you will be able to see yourself in their journeys.

Enjoy!

Note:

Our story is about Lily & Liz.

There is no particular reason our story is about two women.

This concept works for anyone with emotions, regardless if they are male or female.

Look for yourself in their thoughts, behaviors and actions.

Contemplate yourself through their stories.

Learn from their experiences and make the choice to begin driving your bus immediately.

The World of Lily & Liz

Our adventure begins in the town of Now, a beautiful little place nestled into the hills of Awe and Challenges. At the center of Now is a deep lake called Peace. There are extensive walking paths all along the edges of Lake Peace. On the outskirts of the lake, there is a beautiful row of houses on Possibilities Drive. Smack in the middle, we find ourselves at the homes of Lily and Ben, and Liz and Tom. Lily and Liz have known each other since high school, where they became fast friends and have remained that way since. Lily and Liz also work together at the local company in town. Their husbands, Ben and Tom, each own their own business and are also friends.

Lily has always been a cautious optimist. She has an obsession with books and devours them readily. Always up for learning, she rarely reads fiction. She wants to learn something every time she reads, so she studies anything that interests her along with a deep desire to figure herself out. She readily dives into self-help books, continually sharing them with Ben. Even though Ben doesn't seem to be listening, she laughs because she knows that he really is paying attention. Lily's nature is to start each day in a happy frenzy, smiling with frenetic energy. She works hard on finding happiness.

Liz has a different story. Liz grew up in an environment that had her question herself all the time. Liz rarely feels sure of her decisions. She really doesn't have any hobbies other than cooking. Even then, in her cooking, she doesn't like to experiment. Most days, Liz gets up feeling defeated before the day even begins. They seem like an odd couple, Liz and Lily as friends, but they have been for a long time and are a part of each other's lives.

One fateful afternoon, Lily was on a break at work and she came across a link to a video called authorkimjohnson.com/72hourchallenge

Purely out of curiosity, she clicked on the link and viewed the short video. Self-development had always intrigued Lily and she began to wonder if it could be so simple to change herself. During the video, the author challenged the viewers to take a 72-hour challenge. Three days of paying attention to your emotions. Nothing particularly difficult, Lily thought, yet she could see how knowing what was going on behind the scenes in your mind could be extremely helpful.

Quite often in the past, she had come across other programs and challenges for self-development and they were much longer. But 72 hours of consciously committing to choosing the driver of your bus seemed like fun.

Lily decided that she would take on the challenge and read the book. She went onto Amazon and downloaded it to her tablet.

Wherever this adventure would take her, she would give it her all. Plus, if she could get Ben on board, it could be something to help them both.

Every work day, Lily and Liz would drive back and forth together. On this particular day, Liz was the driver. As they got into the car, Lily's enthusiasm was abundant. She immediately began telling Liz all about the challenge. She explained all about her emotions being a cast of characters on a bus in her head. She explained how we could consciously choose who was driving our bus and how that would change the outcome of the moment.

As Lily went on and on, Liz pretended to listen. Liz was longing for the ride to end. *Not another one of Lily's self-help schemes*, she thought.

Just as they pulled into the driveway of Liz's house, Lily said to Liz, "I am going to do this challenge. Would you like to do it with me?" Liz's face was blank. She hated these kinds of questions. She wanted no part of this exercise. She was exhausted and all she wanted to do was go inside and put her pajamas on. At that moment, Lily recognized Liz's expression. "Don't worry about it. It's no big deal," commented Lily. "I'll let you know how it goes and then you can join in if you want to," said Lily.

In a wave of relief, Liz leaned over and gave Lily a hug. "I'll see you in the morning," said Liz. The two friends parted ways and headed off to their separate homes.

When Lily got into her home, she couldn't stop thinking about starting the challenge the next day. She rewatched the video to make sure she understood exactly what she had to do. She really felt like she understood her emotions in general, but she knew that she was not in control all the time. When she started to think about it, she recognized that this was going to be a fascinating experiment for her to do. She had always wanted to be more in control of her choices and emotions. She felt this was the perfect way to do it.

Before Ben arrived home, she decided to do the exercise that was recommended in the video. She grabbed a piece of paper and she started to write out all of her emotions, at least the ones she could identify. Lily thought about her day and what emotions had shown up that were driving her bus. She shook her head and laughed when she realized how many times during this day alone, that Irritated girl had been driving her bus. She thought of herself as a really happy person most of the time, but she knows that at work Irritated Girl shows up.

Lily also realized, as she was writing out her list, how easily Ben could push her buttons. While Lily loves

Ben deeply, she realizes that her energy often overwhelms him. In those moments, she gets very frustrated that he's not paying enough attention to her. Lily decided that she's going to share this exercise with Ben so that he knows what she's doing and he can help give her feedback. With any luck, Ben will want to participate too. Since the book was somewhat of a quick read, which Ben would appreciate, she figured he would be open to join in.

When Ben arrived home, Lily couldn't wait to share what she was doing. As Ben listened to Lily tell the story, he had to admit it sounded like a good idea. He thought to himself about his day and how many clients he had dealt with. He thought about how he had struggled to be patient with a woman who could not understand what he was explaining. When Lily finished, her enthusiasm was radiating. She couldn't contain herself so she asked Ben," What do you think? Do you want to do this with me?" Ben knew that this would be a lot of work for him as any time Lily goes 'all in', she goes 'ALL IN'! There's no question that when she takes something on, she does it 100%. So that meant that if Ben did this with her, she would have the same expectations for him. He really liked the idea though, and he thought it could help him, so with a resounding yes, they agreed to start the next morning. That evening, Lily was powering through the book, learning as much as she could about her emotions.

Over at Liz and Tom's house, Liz was struggling to figure out what to make for dinner. She was frustrated that there were piles of laundry sitting on the floor. She was frustrated that she had to clean her kitchen. It seemed to her that it was like this every day.

She was thinking about what Lily had talked to her about on the way home, but there was no way she was going to do it. It seemed futile. Why should she have to make changes with herself when it wasn't her that was wrong? The more she thought about it, the more she was convinced that it was the people around her that were causing her problems. Tom didn't help enough... Her boss didn't appreciate her workload... even Lily didn't understand. With a deep sigh, Liz walked into her laundry room and started sorting the laundry.

When Tom arrived home, Liz did not greet him with a smile. As she walked past him with a pile of folded clothes, the first words out of her mouth were, "It would be really great if you helped with the laundry at some point."

In a moment of frustration, Tom barked back at her and said, "It would be really great if sometimes you at least said hello to me!" With that, the tone was set for the entire night. There would be no discussion or niceties. At this point, they went on their separate ways. Tom went down to the basement with a beer in his hand. Liz stayed upstairs and had a bowl of cereal for dinner. By the time Liz decided to go to bed, she felt wholly defeated again. The little voice in her head kept asking, *"What is the point of being in a marriage if he is not there to support me?"*

Sadly, she fell asleep with this thought still on her mind.

Day One - The Challenge Begins

Lily's Morning

As Lily's alarm went off, she realized this was the first day of her experiment with who was driving her bus. She remembered immediately that part of this process was to *set yourself up for success* from the moment your eyes opened. So instead of jumping out of bed and beginning all the tasks for her day, she reflected. She closed her eyes again and consciously thought about who she wanted in control of herself right now. *What emotion should she start the day with?* She decided to go with Grateful. If Gratitude was driving her bus, then she knew her day would start differently.

She usually woke up in a very pragmatic state of mind. Only thinking about tasks and getting things done. It was new for her to think about being grateful when nothing had happened to be grateful for yet. In that split second, a thought occurred to her... She was in a warm bed with clean sheets, lying next to her husband that she loved very much. She could hear her dog breathing, lying on the floor beside her. She loved that dog very, very much. The sunshine started to break through the blinds of their bedroom. She realized she was grateful for it being sunny today. She was grateful for just about everything around her. Funny, she had never thought of it like that before.

She reached over and kissed Ben on his forehead. He opened his eyes and asked her if everything was okay because that was not something she usually did. She looked at him and said, "Everything is amazing." She got up out of bed, reached down to give the dog a hug and grabbed her workout clothes. The entire time she was getting ready to take the dog out for their run, she kept thinking about who was driving her bus. She kept thinking how grateful she was that she had the time in the morning to go do a run with her dog. She kept thinking about how excited she was that they had such a nice neighborhood in which to run. All of this was new to her because she was generally on autopilot. She was not happy or unhappy, typically, just being Get Things Done Girl. It was really astounding how quickly she was noticing who was driving now. She realized that choosing the emotion of gratitude throughout her morning was undoubtedly changing the way she felt physically as well as mentally.

As Lily and her dog ran through the neighborhood, she could feel her driver switching back and forth. She was experiencing all kinds of creative thoughts about what she wanted to do over the upcoming weekend. She then realized that it must be Creativity driving her bus. She started thinking about how strong her body felt as she was running. The thought of running the company 5K excited her. All of a sudden, she realized her Competitive Girl was driving the bus.

By the time she got back to her house, Lily had counted five different bus drivers! She wasn't sure if it had been more or not, but she was certain she had counted at least five. She grabbed her notebook and wrote them down: Gratitude. Creativity. Competitive. Curiosity. Inspired. As she wrote down the emotions that were driving her bus so far that morning, she was completely surprised. How could it be that she was experiencing all these different feelings and had never realized what an impact they had? She started to think about how many times she had taken a run with the dog through the neighborhood and never appreciated it. She started thinking about how many times she had got out of bed without thinking about how much she loved Ben. She realized that today was shaping up to be an interesting day.

When Ben came down the stairs and into the kitchen, Lily greeted him with a huge hug and a kiss. She said, "Remember, today's the first day of our bus experiment!"

Ben looked at her and smiled. "I figured that out this morning when you kissed my forehead. I'm all over it with you. While you were out with the dog, I was thinking about how much I appreciated you taking care of yourself as well as the dog. I thought about how grateful I was that I had created this company even though that on some days it drives me insane. When I heard you come back in the door, I thought about how excited I am to spend my life with you."

The look on Lily's face said it all. She was in total shock. Ben had never said anything like that to her before. While he'd always been a tremendously wonderful person and a loving husband, he was not someone to share things like that. Again, Lily thought to herself, *This is going to be a very interesting day.*

At the last minute, as they were getting ready to head out the door, Lily realized that she had forgotten to pack the playgroup bag for the dog. Usually, something like this happening would make Lily fly into a state of panic. She would feel ashamed she had forgotten something, and the stress of not being on time would take over. At that moment, she looked at Ben and said: "I forgot to pack the dog's bag, give me three minutes and I'll have it ready." Instead of letting panic drive her bus, she consciously chose to have calm drive her bus. “If calm is driving my bus, I will able to do this quickly and efficiently. If I let panic drive my bus, I'll move too fast and create even more problems.” Surprisingly, she was able to get everything together quickly and Ben and the dog were out the door along with her, in about five minutes. As she dashed down the driveway to her car, she thought to herself, *If Organized Girl is driving my bus, I will have this dog bag packed the night before, so it's ready to go in the morning. This is great training for when we have kids!* As she laughed to herself, she got in the car and texted Liz that she was ready to go.

Liz's Morning

The morning at Liz's house began quite differently. When her alarm went off, she reached over and hit the snooze button. *Oh no, it can't already be time to get up, thought Liz.* Immediately, she fell back to sleep. 15 minutes later, the second alarm went off. In a state of automatic pilot, Liz hit the snooze button again. She didn't think about the fact that this would cause her grief over the next hour, causing her to become behind schedule. She also didn't think about the fact that Tom hates it every time she hits the snooze button. Tom gets up later than Liz. He also works later than Liz, but she rarely remembers that's the reason why he sleeps in for an extra ninety minutes. The frustrating thing for Tom is that Liz doesn't seem to care about that. He's asked her repeatedly not to let the alarm sound over and over. Liz doesn't care, though.

She likes to set the alarm for the time she would like to get up, but then never does. After hitting the snooze button three times, Liz finally decided to get up. As she sat on the edge of her bed, her dog came over, wagging his tail and looked up at her. "No, I'm not taking you for a walk right now. I don't have time," murmured Liz. She fumbled her way into the bathroom and turned on the shower.

Helplessness was clearly driving her bus. The thoughts running through her head were not resourceful. She did not want to go to the office and she was certainly not looking forward to a day of work. Not when she was this tired. The entire time she was in the shower, she was thinking about things that have been annoying her. Although Liz didn't know it, Annoyed was now driving her bus.

She was thinking about her boss, the piles of paper on her desk, the fact that the lunchroom would smell like fish and how she can't stand that smell. She was even thinking about the fact that Tom was able to sleep an extra 90 minutes and it really irritates her. Liz's entire shower was filled with a steady stream of people and events that irritated her. She barely noticed the water. She showered on autopilot, giving everybody that pops into her head attention. As she dried off and got ready to blow dry her hair, she looked in the mirror and thought, *I can't stand my hair.*

Liz headed downstairs without as much as a glance Tom's way. No kiss goodbye. No "I love you." No "I hope you have a good day." She went down to the kitchen, continuing her internal rant about how they didn't have the cream that she liked for her coffee. Interestingly, the dog kept trying to change her focus. Nudging her, wagging his tail and looking at her for attention the entire time, to no avail because Liz barely noticed he was there.

She grabbed a piece of paper and began to write Tom a note: '*Since you have a more flexible day than I do, make sure you go grocery shopping. We don't have any cream. I don't care what else you get.*'

Just then, her phone buzzed. It was Lily and she was ready to go. Liz thought to herself, *Great. Off to a day at the Hellhole.*

The Ride to Work...

Lily patiently waited in the car for Liz to come out. Just as she was getting ready to text her again, Liz opened the passenger side door and got into Lily's car. It was immediately evident to Lily that Liz was in a bad mood, yet again. "Good morning, Liz!" said Lily, with excitement in her voice. Lily gave Liz a look and mumbled under her breath. She buckled herself in the car and immediately Liz started talking about the experiment. Lily was excited that she was already noticing how she felt and that it was having an immediate shift in her perspective.

Liz sat and listened without comment.

Quite honestly, she did not want to hear what Lily had to say; however, she would listen because of their friendship. Finally, as Lily finished telling her about her observations of the morning, she asked Liz, "Are you sure you don't want to try this with me?" Somewhere deep down inside, Liz did want to try the experiment. Somewhere deep down inside, she believed that she could do it. The truth was that self-doubt and apathy were driving her bus as she was listening to Lily talk.

Self-doubt would not allow her to say that she wanted to try it. So instead, her response was, "I don't know Lily...I guess I'll just watch you do this for the next three days and see what happens. I'll decide after I see what happens with you."

Lily couldn't have been any happier. She knew that a response like that from Liz, albeit not very enthusiastic, was at least a spark.

As they pulled into the parking lot of the office, Lily realized that she did not stress about being late the entire time they were driving. She realized that nearly every day, she was anxious driving to work. She envisioned that they would hit traffic, there would be an accident and they would be late. Today, she did not have one negative thought about the ride. Ironically they did hit traffic. Ironically they did see an accident, but it didn't delay them. As she got out of the car, she realized that Inspired Girl drove them to the office today. She didn't experience, Anxiety and Stress because they had not been driving. She realized that the ride seemed effortless even though the negative events occurred. She realized whomever was driving her internal bus really did control the external journey.

Excitedly, she wanted to point this out to Liz; however, Liz was already way ahead of her and walking into the building. Instead of feeling Frustration for not being able to get through to Liz quicker, Lily decided that she was going to STOP, REFLECT, CHOOSE and REDIRECT her driver before she walked through the door to work. She decided that her driver for today would be curiosity. If she could stay curious all day, she could identify which emotions were trying to hijack her bus when her buttons were being pushed. With an increased level of excitement, she pulled open the door to the office building and entered.

Lily's Day at the Office

The office environment where Lily and Liz work was a lot like other office environments: a mixture of different types of people with different skill sets and lots of varying emotions flying around daily.

Lily and Liz have offices on opposite sides of the hallway. They are on the marketing team, which, in general, experiences a lot of stress and uncertainty. Things seem to change quickly in the world of marketing. What worked at one time, won't work the next time.

Lily and Liz work for Jim. Jim has a lot of responsibility. His marketing department is responsible for bringing in 70% of the leads that come into the company. While Jim is a nice guy most days, it's apparent that he feels the stress from his boss. When he gets stressed, he passes it on to everyone around him. The best thing about Jim though, is he's always willing to listen. When his employees take the time to communicate with him, he will take the time to listen.

As Lily entered her office, she felt a wave of energy come over her. She could see that Jim had left a pile of papers right on her chair for her. This was an indication from him that they are urgent. Normally this would send Lily into a tailspin immediately. But not today. Lily's mind was very clear. *I need to stop, reflect, choose and redirect.*

Immediately, Lily told herself to stop, and she took a deep breath. The next step is to decide who's going to drive. *Who is the best driver for this situation?* She decided that Curiosity would be her best bet. As she learned in the video, she can choose the driver that would serve her best. She then asked the question, *If Curiosity is driving my bus, how would she handle this situation?*

Almost immediately, Lily regained composure. She was no longer victim to an emotional situation that she did not choose. While Jim did give her the extra work, he did not tell her she had to get stressed out doing it. He did not tell her anything. All he actually did was place a big stack of papers on her chair. With Curiosity driving her bus, Lily decided to go through all the papers and see what they entailed. One by one, she sorted through them, deciding what was urgent and what seemed to be able to wait. After she finished going through the papers, Lily had questions for Jim. She picked up all the papers and headed to his office with Curiosity still driving her bus.

This is *very* unlike Lily. Usually, she would sit with the pile of papers feeling overwhelmed and try to figure out what to do. Even though going to Jim's office and questioning him was not something that Lily usually did, she made the decision to do it. Surprisingly, she felt extremely Confident.

As Lily sat with Jim, she explained that she had a number of projects still in the works and while she didn't mind taking on the new projects, these new additions would affect her timelines. With Curiosity again driving her bus, she specifically asked him, “Which jobs would you like me to focus on, Jim? It would help me to know which are the priorities, and what are the hard deadlines?”

Jim smiled. He felt like for the first time, he saw Lily step into a leadership role instead of a supporting role. Jim had absolutely no problem explaining it and telling her he was sorry this all got dumped onto the team. Jim went on to explain the time frames that the office was giving him and they were not his choices, they were directly from his boss. Jim also explained to her that he was willing to go back with the timeline she created for him to see if he could buy any more time.

Lily immediately felt Empowered. She knew she could get help from Jim. All it really took was not defaulting to Aggravated or Frustrated, which would have been the standard reaction. When she stays Curious, she becomes Empowered. Lily recognized this had never happened to her before. On an average day, she would just smile and try to work her way through it.

The shift that was happening within her was tremendous.

Lily headed back to her office and made a decision to timeline everything that she had been working on. She laid it out very simply so that she could see how much time had been invested already and how much time still needed to be spent. She examined everything and then made decisions in regard to her tasks. Within twenty minutes, she had it down on a spreadsheet and was ready to get busy.

For the rest of the morning, Lily felt like she was making tremendous progress. She also made the decision once the timeline was done, to shift from Curiosity driving her bus to Determined driving her bus. She wanted to clear her list as soon as possible and determined it was the best way to go.

By lunch, Lily had a different perspective on the day. She knew it was going to be a busy week, probably a busy month, but she was okay with that. As long as she could manage her emotions, she felt as though she could make it through with flying colors.

Instead of taking her typical approach at lunch and heading to the lunchroom with everyone else, Lily decided to go outside and eat her lunch. It was a gorgeous day; the sun was shining and there was a gentle breeze. As she sat on the bench under the tree, she decided to switch the driver of her bus to Joy. Lily recognized that it had been a long time since she was able to feel Joy while she was at work. The sounds of the birds were something that she rarely noticed, yet today she was hearing them all. Over the course of the forty-five minutes she was outside, her level of awareness had once again heightened. When it was time to go back inside, Lily was recharged. She felt as though she was in an excellent frame of mind for the afternoon.

The rest of the day flew by for Lily.

She had a few moments here and there when she was feeling frustrated, but she repeatedly switched drivers as necessary. Lily actually found this quite comical as she realized throughout her day, she probably had switched drivers at least fifteen times. She even sent herself back to watch the video again to make sure she wasn't doing this incorrectly somehow, wondering if fifteen times was too many. Ironically, she realized that Judgement was driving her bus. “Judgement, when did you hijack my bus?” Lily laughed to herself.

When it was time to go home, Lily walked over to Liz's office and peeked around the corner. "Liz, are you set to go?"

Liz looked up from her desk with a sigh. "I can't wait to get out of here. I really got nothing done today and I'm beyond irritated right now. Give me five minutes and I'll be ready to go."

Liz's Day at the Office

The moment Liz entered her office, she had a complaint. While she did not have a pile of papers sitting on her chair waiting for her like Lily did, she did have a Post-it note stuck on the screen of her computer. 'Make sure you see me early' was written on it. Of course, it was from Jim. She dreaded walking down the hall to his office. She was in no mood for this, although she was never in a mood for this. While Jim really didn't bother her very much, she just didn't like the uncertainty of what was coming her way. She struggled every day with feeling like something unexpected would be thrown her way.

As Liz walked down the hallway, she couldn't help but think about how miserable her morning had been. Today wasn't looking any better. She ran through the scenarios of what Jim could possibly want her for this early in the day.

None of the possibilities flying through her mind seemed very appealing to her. She began to feel her chest get heavy and her throat became dry. By the time she reached Jim's office, she had a sick feeling in her gut. A constant stream of negative thoughts ran through her mind. When she got into Jim's office, he was not there. She sat down in the chair up against the wall and pulled out her phone as a distraction. She started to look through emails, which, unfortunately, made her even more stressed out. She could see that two other people were also looking to meet with her about projects they were deep into working on as well. As Jim walked through the door and said “good morning”, her attention was split between the phone and him. She felt like she was in a fog and unfortunately she was.

"Hey, good morning, Liz! I just wanted to catch up with you on the Hartley project before you went any further. I think you're doing a great job so far and I just wanted to give you some client feedback. They have some small tweaks but nothing major. All in all, I think it should only add about three hours of work. Not so bad considering the size of the project," said Jim.

A steady stream of thoughts ran through Liz's mind. Three hours might not seem like a lot to him, but to her, it was significant.

She completely ignored the fact that he told her that she was doing a great job. She completely ignored the fact that he said the client was happy. She completely ignored the fact that the scope of the project was larger than anything she had worked on previously and she had made tremendous progress to that point.

Panic was driving Liz's bus. Yes, panic. What that meant was all Liz could hear was that three hours of additional work had been added to her schedule. She felt her face turn red with irritation.

"Jim, three hours of additional work, on top of what I already have on the other projects... I don't know where it's going to come from. I am already overburdened and then to ask me to take on additional changes and three more hours is not only unfair, but it's unreasonable. I've worked my butt off on this project and I have no idea how I'm going to add in three more hours." Liz complained.

Jim was taken aback by her response. He recognized that his team was overworked. However, Jim had always told them to let him know well before they hit the breaking point. The truth was that he had always been someone that would figure out a solution with them when they asked. Jim has also recognized over the last year that Liz had become increasingly moody. He noted that she couldn't manage concurrent projects and he had purposely limited the number of items he put on her plate, but this was the nature of their business. Sometimes it gets chaotic. More importantly, if she had come to him before she felt so overwhelmed, he could have brought in an assistant to help.

"Liz, I'm very sorry that you feel this way. I can see that I've upset you and that was not my intent. I wanted you to know that you were doing a great job. You seem to have overlooked all of those points. Why don't we take this back up after lunch today and we will figure out a way to get you some help on the additional work," said Jim.

By this point, Liz was so entrenched in her anger that she stood up and walked out the door without a word. As she walked down the hall to her office, she was overwhelmed with Confusion, Anxiety, Anger and Frustration. She thought about going over to talk to Lily but then decided against it. *What's the point?* She thought to herself. *Lily always has a bright outlook on everything and she's going to tell me we will figure it out. I don't need to hear that this time.* She went back to her office, sat down and began to work again.

For the next four hours, Liz struggled to concentrate. Her thoughts kept looping back to what was wrong and the narrative that she had created in Jim's office. She kept running the scenario over and over and over again. By the time lunch arrived, Liz was exhausted. She decided to go sit in the corner of the lunchroom, eat lunch and play on her phone. So far, this day was exactly what she had expected.

By the time the afternoon was over, Liz was drained. The meeting after lunch with Jim was somewhat alleviating. He had arranged for her to share an assistant with another coworker. It would be short-term assistance over the next few weeks. Jim felt that this would give Liz the help she needed on the Hartley project, as well as to help her clean up the details of some other projects she was working on. Jim was hoping that this would smooth everything over.

The reality was different, though. Liz was angry that it took Jim so long to give her an assistant. She was focused on her feeling that everyone gets too much work. She was focused on the belief that there was no end in sight.

When the assistant popped into her office to say "hello" and that she was looking forward to helping her out, Liz's greeting was less than enthusiastic. She gave her a flat synopsis of the work that had to be done. She did not seem grateful at all for the help.

At this point, one can only imagine what the assistant was thinking.

This day would end as most days; Liz was exhausted and was packing work to take home. Her inability to focus during the day on anything other than her irritation and anger robbed her of the time she could have spent being more productive. As she put her bag over her shoulder to walk out the door and meet Lily at the car, Liz thought to herself, *This just sucks...I can't catch a break. Now I've got to work on this all night long. I have a whole new understanding for the term rat race now.*

The Ride Home

When Lily got to the car, she lowered the windows and turned the music on. She sat back in the seat and let the sunshine cover her face. She started to think that today was a great day. She began to envision all the wonderful things that came her way as she worked very hard to maintain clarity and consciously make decisions on who was driving her bus. She recognized that as she sat there, and she thought about all of this, she started to feel even better. Suddenly she thought to herself, "It's really amazing how I can change my own emotional state by focusing on something different."

Liz made her way out to the car. Her body felt heavy and she couldn't wait to get into the car. As she opened the door and slumped into the seat, a sense of relief started to wash over her. She realized it was just being out of the building and office itself that made her feel better. She looked at Lily and said," I am so glad this day is over" and rolled her eyes. All she could think about was getting home and putting on her pajamas.

Lily started to ask questions but could see that Liz was in no mood to talk. That kind of bummed her out because she really wanted to talk about all the significant distinctions she had made today. However, she certainly didn't want to make Liz feel bad about herself by talking about her own wins. So Lily sat there and said nothing.

Liz however, was extremely relieved that Lily was not talking. She was hoping that Lily would get the hint and not talk about anything happy. It wasn't that Liz couldn't talk about happy things; it was just that Lily seemed to always try to find cheery things to talk about, which got under Liz's skin. She would think to herself that Lily's life couldn't possibly be that great. *We have the same job,* she would contemplate. But that didn't matter right now. She was just grateful that it was quiet.

When they were almost home, Lily looked over at Liz and said, “Do you guys have plans for tonight?”

Almost immediately, Liz felt resistant. She didn't want to talk about what would happen when she got home. It was Thursday night and most Thursday nights were frustrating for her. Tom would always come home later than usual and that meant that the dog walk, dinner and chores were all on her. She didn’t know how to respond to Lily’s question. She didn't want her to know how much she didn't enjoy being with her husband as of late.

Even though they were friends, she didn't want to talk about it.

Reluctantly, Liz turned to Lily and said, "My Thursday nights are usually difficult because Tom gets home late. This means everything falls into my lap and it's not really a fun night for me."

Lily looked at her and said, "I'm sorry that happens for you." She gently reached over and put her hand on Liz's leg. "If there's anything I can do to help you tonight, just let me know."

As they pulled into Lily's driveway, anyone could see the difference in the moods between the two of them. Lily was excited to be home. She jumped out of the car, reached in the back and grabbed her things, almost skipping around the car.

Liz looked drained and heavy. As they parted ways, Liz gave Lily a half smile as Lily blew her a kiss.

Lily's Evening

As Lily walked into her house, she was greeted by her dog. Lots of wiggling and excitement always made Lily smile. To this day, she couldn't believe how much the dog loved her and would get excited every time she came into the house. She didn't grow up with a dog and she hadn't understood the kind of unconditional love they offer. This dog had changed her whole world. She kneeled down on the floor and said, "I am so happy to see you! Let me get my sneakers on and we will go for a walk!"

Lily ran up the stairs, changed her clothes, put her hair up in a ponytail, filled her water bottle and out the door they went. As they walked around the lake, Lily decided this would be a great time to continue to practice what she had learned in the video.

She started to think about who was driving her bus today. She began to wonder who was driving now as they walked. She realized that Get Things Done Girl was driving her bus right now. This distinction somewhat shocked her. She has always loved walking the dog because it made her get up and move. So what was the reason that 'Get Things Done Girl' was in her mind as her driver right now?

As she walked, she wondered and she realized that being able to cross the walk off of her list of things to do was incredibly important to her. She really likes to cross things off of her list.

The moment she realized this, she decided to practice STOP, REFLECT, CHOOSE, REDIRECT.

What driver would she like to have right now? She thought about enjoying the walk and how that would be the best choice. She envisioned herself switching drivers to the Mindful Girl. If Mindful Girl were driving the bus, that would mean that she was in the moment, enjoying every aspect of the walk. She focused on choosing Mindful Girl. She began to enjoy the warm afternoon sunshine on her face. She noticed the breeze slightly blowing her dog's ears.

It quickly became evident to her that this was not as easy as she initially thought it would be. Her mind kept thinking about things to do as her Get Things Done Girl kept stealing the wheel of the bus. She laughed to herself and realized that this was going to take practice for sure! Lily worked hard on the redirecting for the entire 45-minute walk.

During that time, she had to keep taking the wheel back to Mindful Girl. Interestingly, Mindful Girl made Lily notice things she had not noticed in a very long time. She began to see how much the hiking trail was changing this season. She noticed how many flowers were still blooming. She noticed how happy the dog was. For that matter, she noticed how happy she was.

Throughout the walk, even though it was challenging to keep catching herself, she realized for the first time how much time she spent in her head and not living in the moment. As she walked back up the steps to the house, Ben pulled into the driveway. She looked at him with a big huge smile on her face and decided to walk down and give him a big hug and a kiss. He immediately smiled at her and said: "I don't know what I did to deserve that, but I'm sure happy I got it!" Lily chuckled to herself. She realized the moment he pulled up, she was thinking about how much she loved him and not thinking about how many chores they had to do in the house. She really appreciated Ben and wanted him to know that.

As they walked into the house together, Lily knew tonight would be different because she would be different.

Throughout the rest of the night, Lily and Ben chatted about what Lily was learning. She told Ben about how her day had been different because she had been seeing the day differently, or better yet feeling the day differently.

She explained how many times she caught herself and how just mere observation of who was driving her bus while she was walking the dog, made the experience completely different.

As Ben took it all in, he recognized how often he did this too. He made a commitment to himself that he was going to work on doing this as well. He thought to himself if Lily could do it and commit to working so hard at it, he wanted to join her with it.

When they finished eating dinner, instead of Lily getting upset about how many things she still had to do, she looked at Ben and said, "If I was to make a list of all the things that have to be done tonight, would you be willing to split them up with me so we could get done sooner and I could spend some time with you?"

Ben looked at her and said without question, "Yes! I have just one request. Will you allow me to do the chores the way I want to do them, as opposed to the way you want them done? I'm happy to help. I just don't want to have you follow me around and re-do what I'm doing because I'm not doing it the “right way."

At that moment, Lily realized how she did that all the time. In that split second, she recognized how that must make Ben feel. What a horrible way to make somebody feel when they are trying to help you!

She walked over to him, looked in his eyes and said, "I am so sorry that I do that. I understand why I do that now. That is Certainty Girl driving my bus. She's the one that likes to make sure everything is done the right way, well at least my right way. I know she has a place and she's good at what she does, she's just not good when I'm with you. I promise you tonight I will not say a word and I will be appreciative and happy with what you are doing to help me."

She could see Ben's face light up instantaneously. He leaned down and he gave her a kiss and said, "Let's get all this done, where's the list?"

Over the next hour, they got the bathrooms cleaned, the kitchen cleaned, the laundry all sorted with a load in the washer and a load in the dryer, vacuuming upstairs and downstairs, as well as even cutting the dog's toenails.

Lily started thinking to herself when she saw how much they got done, how foolish she had been. Sure, she could notice that Ben's vacuuming wasn't precisely the way hers was, but she was focused on being mindful and enjoying the moment. She was focused on letting him know how much she appreciated him. The few spots that Ben missed didn't matter. What mattered was that her workload had been cut in half and she wasn't trying to control every little aspect of their evening. What mattered was she actually was enjoying what she was doing. The so-called chores were no longer feeling like chores.

When they finished everything, Ben said, "Are you up for watching a movie and having a glass of wine with me?"

As Lily looked down at her watch, she realized there was plenty of time to do that before she had to go to bed. She couldn't remember the last time that she felt that way. She immediately smiled at Ben and said, "Absolutely! ...and I want to thank you for being patient with me. I don't mean to show up like a control freak and I realize it's not healthy for me or for us. I'm not letting her drive my bus anymore, well at least when I can recognize she's driving!" she said laughingly.

Over at Liz's House...

As Liz walked away from the car, she realized that she was not being a good friend. She knew she was acting like a Negative Nelly, but she couldn't do anything about it. She walked over to the mailbox and grabbed the mail. Even though the sun was shining and it felt really wonderful on her back, she was focused on everything that was wrong. As she walked up to her front door and put the key in, she took a deep breath and thought to herself, Please, oh please, let the kitchen be clean, as she pushed the door open. The next five minutes seemed like a blur. She dropped her bags on the kitchen counter and walked around the house looking for everything that was wrong. A toilet that hadn't been flushed, dishes in the kitchen sink, clothes piled on the kitchen table...to her, the list was endless.

The entire time she was inspecting the house, her dog was trying to get her attention. Happily wagging his tail and dancing around her, he went completely unnoticed. Eventually, he stopped trying and walked over and sat down next to his food bowl. When Lily noticed him, she snapped at him, "I know you're hungry. I'll get to it in a minute!"

Liz began to speak to herself out loud and yell. She was feeling overwhelmed with all the things she had found. The entire time, a constant dialogue in her head was running about why Tom didn't help out.

She was thinking over and over that it was not fair that he left her to do all of this by herself. She remembered complaining to him about this just a few days ago and yet today the same circumstances happened again. In a moment of Anger, she decided it would be great to not do any of it. "Screw it! I'm not doing any of this!" She went upstairs and put on her yoga pants and a T-shirt, grabbed her sneakers, called the dog and said, "We're going for a really long walk right now." She decided that she felt so bad she couldn't stay in the house for another second. So off they went, walking the entire lake trail in the neighborhood and then some.

By the time Liz and the dog arrived back at home, it was getting dark. Tom's van was in the driveway, so Liz knew he had run into the mess. But hell, he had made a lot of that mess! As they walked up the path, she was ready for an argument. She was prepared to say whatever she needed to say to make him realize this was not going to continue. She wasn't sure how to approach him; however, she was certainly sure that she was done.

As she walked in the door, Tom was sitting on the couch. Immediately she thought, *How the hell can he just be on the couch sitting there doing nothing?* As Tom went to say hello to her, she put her hand up as if to stop him. She quickly glanced around to see that not much had changed in the house.

In fact, the only changes to the house were the additions of a large pizza and a six pack of beer sitting on the kitchen counter. Before Tom could even tell her that he brought home pizza and beer for dinner for them because he knew she would have been stressed after this long day, Liz began to bark at him. "How the hell can you just sit on that couch while this house is a mess and not even try to help me clean it up?”

Immediately, Tom felt defeated. He put his head down and didn't say a word. Liz began to go on a rant that lasted about ten minutes straight. She brought up things that happened months ago, adding them into her list of current grievances.

She did not notice that Tom just sat there taking it. He wondered if she even cared about how he felt. The truth was, he had seen all of the mess. He even knew he had created part of this mess. He had brought the pizza home hoping that they could have some pizza and beer and then he knew she would want to do some cleaning. He had honestly wanted to help.

But because Liz was so committed to her own perspective of what happened and how it happened, she didn't consider any other possibilities. She was angry and therefore she was going to stay angry. She was not going to tolerate this anymore.

By the end of Liz's rant, Tom had got up from the couch and went to the sink and started doing dishes. He looked exhausted like he had just lost his best friend. Liz, on the other hand, was running around frantically trying to get as much done as she possibly could.

When Tom tried to stop her and explained that he had thought they would eat first and then he would help, she barked at him and said, "I don't believe you. You had no intention of helping. You were just going to eat pizza and drink beer. You would have sat there all night and let me do everything. I'm sick of this, Tom!"

With that, Tom picked up his keys and walked out the front door. Liz began to follow him and asked: "Where are you going?"

Tom turned around and said, "Anywhere that I can get some peace and quiet." Tom walked to his van and left.

As Liz stood on the porch of their house watching him drive away, she felt a sinking pit in her stomach. She was consumed with the fact that she would have to do all of this work herself and completely missed out on the fact that maybe, just maybe, he was telling the truth.

For the next two hours, Liz cleaned her house and did chores that had been long overdue and she would not get to any of the work she brought home. The entire time she was crying and talking to the dog. All she could think to herself was, *How could my life have gone so wrong? How could I have picked such a poor partner? How did I get myself into this mess?*

By the time she finished the tasks, Tom was still not back home. She texted him to see where he was, but he did not answer. For one split second, she thought to herself, *Was I too hard on him?* She decided that it was not worth thinking about any longer and she put her on her pajamas and went to bed.

The last thoughts that were going through her mind were that she was frustrated, sad and that this was never going to get any better. As she drifted off to sleep, she wondered what she had done to deserve this.

Day Two - The Challenge Is Underway

Friday Morning at Lily's House...

Lily woke up five minutes before her alarm went off. As she lay there in bed, she thought to herself. *I never wake up early. I have no idea how I just woke up without the alarm waking me up.*

Thoughts of how Gratitude Girl would handle waking up started to flow through her mind. She began to be thankful for the sheets on her bed. She thought about how much she appreciated being warm. Next, she reached over and lightly touched Ben's back. She began to think about how much she loved him and how he was always so strong for her. She thought about the times that he had shown up for her, like when he had helped her through the tragedy of her mother dying. Just then the cat jumped up onto the bed. It was always funny to Lily how the cat knew precisely when she was supposed to get up. Instead of immediately jumping up like she usually would do, she started to pet the cat and found herself relaxing. She began to have gratitude for how much she loved her cat. It was such a strange feeling for her to be relaxing in the morning, knowing she had to get to work.

When her alarm finally did go off, Lily had realized something. That simple five minutes spent contemplating with Gratitude Girl driving her bus, even before her feet hit the floor, had given her a wave of different energy in her body.

She got up without anxiety and without thinking about all the things that had to be done. She leaned over and kissed Ben good morning. Since it was Friday, Lily was headed out to her CrossFit class. She quickly got her clothes on, grabbed her water bottle and was out the door. The entire drive over to her class, Lily focused on how she wanted to break through the barriers that she had felt while being in the class. Since she had started going to CrossFit, she always felt like she was much weaker than other people in the class. She couldn't do the physical things that other women in the class could do and it made her feel weak.

Her entire life, she had thought about her limitations. Since she started doing the three-day challenge, she was becoming increasingly aware of who was driving her bus. To her continued surprise, she was shocked at just how much time she spent in the past. As she was running through her thoughts about how struggling through class made her feel, she recognized that it was Judgement who is driving her bus. She wondered how often Judgement had been holding her back. She wondered how much Judgement had made her feel inferior throughout her entire life. Her eyes began to tear up as she thought about the limitations that Judgement had put on her.

In that moment she made a choice.

As she pulled into the parking spot at the CrossFit gym, she said to herself, "Right now, I choose to have Determined Girl walk through that door and kick this class in the ass."

She grabbed her water bottle and got out of the car. She felt completely empowered. No matter what happened in that class, she was not going to judge herself.

As class began, she felt Determined was still driving her bus. This class was always a challenge and today was no exception. She felt her muscles ache and she felt her breath become shallow. This is where Judgement jumped in the seat. But this time, Lily was ready. She said "no way" to herself and promptly put Determined Girl back in the driver's seat. Astonishingly, she had to do this consciously at least ten times. Each and every time however, it became a little bit easier and a little bit quicker. By the end of the class, she was completely saturated with sweat and wholly satiated with gratitude for the fact that she had finished the class feeling like she had won a medal. Judgement was not present. Determined Girl felt over the moon for just accomplishing the class without having to walk to the side and step out.

As Lily got back into her car to head home, she realized that it was not even 7 AM yet and she had to switch drivers at least twenty times. Again she had to remind herself about the video she watched initially, the author had explained that this was part of the process. There's no need to say that you're wrong for slipping into the old emotions. The emotions are just part of the process.

We are human beings and we are emotional creatures. The most important part of this process is to recognize that emotions are here to serve you and give you information. As Lily drove home, she wondered what Judgement was really trying to teach her. What was the reason that Judgement showed up so often for her?

When Lily arrived home from the gym, Ben was in the kitchen just returning from walking the dog. Immediately, she realized how often she would judge the state of the kitchen as she walked in. She would always look for how big the mess was and stress out about having to clean it up. This happened before any other thought came into her head. Once again, Judgement Girl was driving and she realized that Frustration Girl was sitting right behind Judgement girl. However, today she will make a better choice.

She consciously chose Love at that moment. What would her reaction be if Love was driving, she thought? Instantly, her face went from a grimace to a smile. Immediately, Ben's face lit up. He looked at her and said, "You must have had a great workout!"

Lily laughed and said, "Actually, I feel like I got my butt kicked." She leaned over and gave him a kiss and thought about how grateful she was for him. Her mind became curious as she wondered how many times she walked in this kitchen and instantly was angry for absolutely no reason at all. How could simply having a few dishes in the sink make her so angry? She looked over at Ben and said, "I'm off to go shower and I would love to figure out something fun that we can do tonight or tomorrow, something different, and I would love for it to be a suggestion that you make." she said with a chuckle.

Ben began to laugh. His mind immediately began to think of all the things that he would like to do that he knew Lily would probably not want to do. He looked at her and said, "Are we talking my kind of things or your kind of things"?

Lily had already anticipated that question and was ready. "I no longer want it to be my thing or your thing. I would love there to be our things. I'm willing to broaden my horizons and try different adventures. Let's see what we can do that we both love to do. Do you think you can come up with something?"

Without hesitation, Ben answered, "Absolutely!"

With that, Lily was off to shower and get ready for work. As Lily walked up the stairs, she made a commitment that the rest of the morning she was going to have Creativity and Joy driving her bus.

As Lily jumped in the shower, she remembered part of the video she had watched about the 72-hour Challenge. The author had referenced how many times the shower had made her crazy, joking about how many people actually were in the shower with her. Lily decided to really make it a point to pay attention to this. As she showered, she also realized she had endless numbers of people parading through her shower, along with countless numbers of chores running running through her mind. How could this be? How could something as relaxing and enjoyable as a shower be filled with so many people and so many tasks that her mind felt encumbered? She wondered how often her showers were filled with uninvited guests.

As funny as this may sound, she recognized that this was very true for her.

She wondered how many other people did this very thing every day and had no idea what was going on? No wonder everyone showed up at work exhausted and apathetic before their days even started! Once again, giving herself grace, Lily committed that she would be working on staying in the present moment. Slowly but surely it became crystal clear to her that this was something she had to really work on. She realized how much the human mind drifted. It was a human problem, not just a Lily problem.

Over the next thirty minutes, Lily finished getting ready and continued to redirect the drivers in her head. At one point, she even laughed to herself, thinking about all the shenanigans that were taking place.

This was a whole new world to her as well as a completely new understanding of herself. The humor of it all is not lost on her, even though she understood that this was real work.

By the time Lily was ready to walk out to the car and meet Liz, she had lost count of how many times she had to redirect herself. She thought, "No wonder I get so stressed out!"

Lily grabbed her phone and texted Liz that she was on her way out to the car. She took a deep breath and prepared herself in case Liz was not in a good mood. She wished that she could help Liz because she knew Liz was hurting. Lily also knew that one has to want help, and Liz was not there yet. She scooped up her bags and went out the door and to the car.

Friday Morning over at Liz's House...

Liz vaguely heard the alarm the first time it went off. She pushed the snooze button and went immediately back to sleep. By the fourth time the alarm went off, she knew she had to get out of bed. Her body was still exhausted. As she lay there, she thought about how much the day was going to suck. Even though it was Friday, she knew how pressure packed Fridays could be. Then she remembered her fight with Tom. *Ugh,* she thought to herself. She knew she had been harsh, but she couldn't seem to stop. *I will have to deal with this later,* she thought.

She longed for Saturday morning when she didn't have to hear the alarm and could retreat into her own world. All she could think about right now was drinking coffee. She got out of bed and felt her body aching from head to toe. Her thoughts diverted to the fact that her mattress was old. Maybe that was her problem, she needed a new mattress. More money to be spent that she didn't want to spend.

She meandered downstairs as the dog followed her, hoping to go for a walk. She was not in the mood to take the dog for a walk and immediately put him in the backyard, then off to the kitchen she went to make coffee. She picked up her phone on the way and began checking her emails. She had heard countless times that checking emails as soon as you got up was not a good practice. It only adds stress to your day before your day begins. It didn't change her mind though as she grabbed her phone and began scrolling through all of her emails, followed by her text messages, followed by Instagram. Before she knew it, twenty minutes had disappeared and she still hadn't had a cup of coffee. She glanced at the clock and realized the dog was still outside and she was now running behind schedule. "Dammit," she yelled as she ran to let the dog in.

Now the race was on! She had to rush to get everything done because she went to bed without preparing for the next day. She wasn't sure what she wanted to wear. She wasn't sure where her shoes were, and she certainly wasn't sure where her keys were. "Well, this can't get much worse." She said out loud. Just that moment, Tom passed her in the hallway.

After last night's fiasco, he was not going to contend with her at all. He knew to stay out of the way. Tom had learned long ago that when Liz was in a mood, there was no changing her focus. The best thing he could do was avoid her. So instead of saying good morning, he put his head down and continued to walk by.

Unfortunately for Liz, this scene happened often. Tom and Liz fight. Well, Liz yells and Tom retreats. Tom avoids Liz until Liz seems capable of hearing Tom again. Tom then tries to make it better and Liz tries to find a way to feel better. They come back to the middle and are not really happy, but at least they are not fighting. That is until the next triggered event happens. Then the cycle repeats itself over and over.

Liz was sure that Tom has just stopped loving her. She immediately made it all about something other than what was really going on. It never occurred to her that her mood was affecting Tom so much. Ultimately, that was the problem for Liz. Nothing was considered that was outside of her myopic perspective. She chose to see the world from the emotion SHE was feeling. She did not try to learn from what was going on around her. She continued to take in the world as if it was out to get her.

As they passed each other in the hallway, Anger grabbed the wheel of her bus and she started to feel like she wanted to scream. The only thought going through Liz's mind was, *Why does he continue to ignore me? Doesn't he remember what happened last night?* Again, it never occurred to Liz that her mood or reactions were having a profound effect on Tom. Liz was operating with a complete lack of awareness. In fact, Awareness on her bus was sitting so far in the back-it may as well had not been there at all.

Liz threw her phone down on her bed, scurried into the bathroom and turned the shower on. Throughout the course of her shower, she got more and more irritated and angry about Tom's actions. She kept running through past arguments that happened years ago. She kept running through instances when she was angry and he sat there with his head down. She kept thinking about what a "bad" husband he was. The entire time she was in the shower, Liz was in a negative state. The funny thing about this was she felt completely justified. She didn't even realize that she was ramping herself up. She didn't even think about how she didn't get to enjoy her shower. She didn't appreciate the fact that she had hot water in her life. She didn't appreciate the fact that she had soap. She certainly didn't appreciate the fact that she had a beautiful master bathroom in which to shower.

All of the points of gratitude she could have focused on to reset her state of mind and frame of reference did not show up. She was committed to her outrage.

From the perspective of outrage, she made a decision that she was going to say something to Tom. She was going to call him out on his behavior again that morning because she couldn't take it for one more minute. She decided that she would do it right away. If he wasn't going to bring up last night, then she would. She threw her robe on and didn't even bother to dry off completely. She went running down the stairs to find the house empty.

Tom got up and out of the house early, without saying a word.

She stood there for a moment, somewhat shocked, and said out loud, "What the hell? How could he leave without even saying a word to me? Not even goodbye?" Once again, she had made it all about her.

Liz had a pit in her stomach. She rushed back up the stairs to get herself together. She wrestled through her clothes, which were in a big pile at the bottom of her closet because she doesn't take the time to get organized. She pulled out the least wrinkled items she could find. Quickly she threw them on, ran in the bathroom, brushed her teeth and threw her hair up into a bun.

She had one fleeting moment of Gratitude driving her bus -the fact that they had a dog door. This way, she didn't have to stop and walk the dog. Just that moment, Lily texted her that she was on her way out to the car and was ready to leave. Liz thought, *Great, here we go,* and scurried out the door.

The Ride to Work...

By the time Liz got out to the car, Lily had the music on and was all settled in. Liz felt horrible and she knew she looked that way too. Lily was working very hard at not asking questions. Liz was visibly upset and Lily knew that asking questions would only make it worse.

"Good morning," Lily said to Liz with a big smile on her face.

Liz looked back at her with a somewhat astonished look and said, "Morning" in a very flat tone.

Lily just couldn't help herself, even though she knew Liz was not open to it and said, "If there's anything I can do to help you, Liz, all you have to do is ask. I know you're not happy and I can see it on your face and I wish that you would let me help you."

Liz hurried to put her sunglasses on. Her eyes began to well up with tears and she could feel her face getting red. She was on the verge of a breakdown. "Lily, the best thing we could do right now is just not talk about it," Liz said. She could feel her face getting redder by the moment and she knew she needed to compose herself before she got into the office. "I need to just get myself together and I'm a real mess," Liz said with her voice shaking.

Lily had such an urge to talk to her about the concept of *Who's Driving your Bus*, but she knew then was not the time. She knew if she tried to introduce it to her in a moment of despair that it would not work. So she simply said, “Okay, I understand. When you're ready to talk, let me know and if you need me throughout the day, I will always be here."

Lily turned the music up in the car and the conversation stopped. When they got to work, Lily made sure that she helped Liz get settled in. As she walked out of Liz’s office, she thought, *I'm going to send you a big mental hug because I know you need it desperately.*

Lily's Day at the Office – Day 2

As Lily got into her office and settled in, she realized she was focused on the pain that Liz was in. She was not doing a great job of managing herself because she had gone and fallen into someone else's emotions.

Last night, she had read about the concept of falling into someone else's emotions. She'd initially thought that she didn't do that, but here she was, right in someone else's drama. She sat at her desk and took a big drink of water. She thought to herself, *"STOP, REFLECT, CHOOSE, REDIRECT."*

She actually said out loud to herself, "Time to change drivers!" She stood up and walked around her desk and sat back down again and said, "Organizational Girl is in control right this moment!" With that, she began her day.

She had piles and piles of papers on her desk to sort through for this project and she dove in. While her office was quiet and she could get focused on what she needed to do, she recognized that her bus kept getting hijacked. Quite honestly, she was not prepared for how many times she had to reclaim her emotions. She was under the impression that this was going to be somewhat easy. She thought she had a decent level of awareness in her life.

As her morning progressed, she realized that emotion was attached to nearly everything that she touched. She would look at the papers she was sorting through and emotion would show up. Each client had a different framework of emotion that they created in her. Each task had its own unique spin as well. She started to make a list and jot down all the different emotions she was experiencing because she was truly taken aback by how many different ones were showing up for her as well as how often they switched roles.

By the time lunchtime arrived, Lily had a reasonably good understanding of how her emotions were affecting her progress. She didn't have a good handle on controlling them and staying in the emotion she wanted, but she did have a good understanding of the need to choose your bus driver.

She looked down at her watch and realized that she had been in her office three and a half hours and no one else had bothered her. Fridays tended to be very quiet anyway, but this was really interesting.

The night before, she had thought to herself that she wanted to have a lovely quiet morning and she had even mentioned that to Ben. Lo and behold, it happened.

In those three and a half hours, she had completed more work than she realized. She felt as though she had gotten more done than she had all week! Lily grabbed her bag and decided to eat lunch outside where it was warm and sunny.

As she walked down the hall, she stopped by Liz's office and asked her if she wanted to join her outside. Much to her surprise, Liz said yes.

Liz's Day at the Office – Day 2

As Liz entered her office, she became acutely aware of a strange odor. It began to consume her thoughts and she didn't think she would be able to stay in her office. She started looking through her things to figure out what the awful stench was. As soon as she got to the wastebasket by her door, she realized that she had left half of a chicken salad sandwich inside. The smell made her sick. She took the trash to the dumpster and came back to clean up her office. She thought to herself that if she cleaned the office, maybe she would feel better.

The problem was that there was so much disarray that it would take her a full week of doing only organizing to get out of the weeds. She sighed and sat back in her chair. *How could my life be so messed up?* was the thought that kept running through her head. Over and over everything she touched made her feel burdened and irritated. Her phone kept ringing, but she refused to answer and kept letting it go to voicemail. She could hear people talking outside of her office and she could hear the buzz of everyone working, but she didn't want to partake in it. She wondered if anyone would even come to see if she was there but hoped that they wouldn't. Fridays tend to be a day where everybody got caught up and she was hoping that this Friday would be no different.

Liz found her mind constantly wandering back to her argument with Tom. In fleeting moments, she questioned herself on what happened. Was he as rude as she thought? Did he really not love her? Was she the one that was wrong? The ideas and iterations swirled in her mind like a tornado. All the papers on her desk and work table were a reminder of how little she was getting done. The clock seemed as slow as it did when she was in 5th grade as she would wait for the bell to ring. She needed to read every sentence in the document she was working on three or four times to comprehend it. "Ugh," Liz said out loud. "This day could not suck more than it does." She began eating candy out of the jar on her desk. This was never a good sign. Candy was and always has been her 'sad' food. Even though she knew that she would feel HORRIBLE after she ate it, she continued. "I might as well complete the crappy day," she muttered as she shoved a handful into her mouth.

Just then, Lily popped her head into Liz's office. "How about some sunshine for lunch?" Lily asked.

In a moment of desperation, Liz answered, "Hell, yes." Liz picked up her lunch bag and they walked outside together.

Lunch

Liz could feel that Lily really wanted to talk about her challenge, so she actually initiated the conversation; mostly because she didn't want to talk about herself and slightly because she was curious.

"So tell me, Lily, how is your 72-hour challenge going?"

Lily was quite shocked that Liz would ask her, but she was excited to talk about it.

"Well, I will tell you what! I am learning a heck of a lot about myself and I am learning that I have less control over who is driving my bus then I thought I did!"

Lily went on to explain to Liz all the times she caught herself in an emotion that she had not actively chosen. She explained all the challenges she was having maintaining the chosen emotion that she wanted to be driving her bus. In fact, she even shared with Lily about how baffled she was that no one had ever discussed this concept with her in the past.

As Lily talked, Liz listened intently. She could see that Lily was excited and was learning a lot and there was part of it that intrigued her. She had never tried anything like this before, but she could see that her friend felt she was making progress. Up until this point, Liz had not mentioned the fight that she had with Tom. She just didn't want to talk about it and she wasn't sure how to bring it up. She started to see as Lily was describing what was going on for herself, how her own drivers had taken over. It was almost 1 o'clock and she had still not heard from Tom. No text, no phone call. As they finished their lunch and were headed back into the building, Liz decided to text Tom. She thought to herself, *Let's keep this simple – 'I'm sorry'* she typed and hit send. She and Lily walked into the building and back to finish their day.

As they parted ways to go back to their offices, Lily reminded Liz to be patient with herself.

"Liz, none of this is easy, I mean it's really simple when you think about it, but it's just not easy."

"Thank you for saying that," said Liz. "The hardest thing for me is that I'm struggling everywhere right now. I mean we really don't talk about my life with Tom, but it's not just work. I mean, it's me. I mean, I'm not sure what I mean anymore. Whatever I mean, thank you for being there for me even when I'm not nice," said Liz.

Lily just smiled at her and said, "I love you no matter what and you should always remember that. You are my friend and I am here for you."

Lily's Afternoon at the Office - Day 2

Lily went to her office and sat down. She had a sense of Joy after her interaction with Liz. Liz was acting in a way that Lily had never seen before and that made her feel hopeful. Curiously, she searched through her present emotions. She felt joy, love, and understanding. They seem to keep coming one by one. The best part was that she could identify them with ease when she reflected. Understanding that there was a simple way to do this was changing Lily.

As the afternoon progressed, Lily found herself aware of the fact that she was becoming more productive. She was beginning to notice that there had been so many distractions in her head before, it was no wonder it took her so long to accomplish things. The more she became aware of the distractions, the easier it was for her to stop them from taking over. Previously, a simple request for information from someone in her office would cause her to become flustered. The moment Flustered began driving her bus, everything else took longer.

She also began to notice that certain emotions caused more significant distractions. If the emotion was intense, the distraction was longer. If the emotion was just a mere blip, the distraction was much easier to get around. She knew that she would want to share all of this with Jim at some point in time. If everyone was aware of what was going on in their head and who was driving their bus, the office could become much more efficient and a much happier place overall. However, that thought in and of itself right now was a distraction and she laughed to herself. "I need to stay on course to finish everything that I want to accomplish by the end of the day."

Over the next four hours, her day flew by. By the time she looked at her watch again, it was almost 4:45! This distinction of time really resonated with her. She often felt like days dragged by and that she couldn't wait for them to be over. Without thinking about it much, she was a clock watcher. She was aware of the time seemingly every half hour. However, not today. This thought made her curious... Would this become a new habit for her? Not checking the clock? She never thought that was possible except now everything seemed possible. And for a fleeting moment, she thought, *It appears that my entire life is controlled by that emotion and the thoughts related to it. What if my perspectives have been so far off that they had actually been holding me back? Wow. I am and have been my own worst enemy.* With that, she grabbed her phone and texted Liz. It was time to pack up and go home to enjoy the weekend.

Liz's Afternoon - Day 2

As Liz entered her office, her phone vibrated in her hand. She looked down and it was a text from Tom. It said, "I know. I'm sorry too." A wave of relief came over Liz as she realized how grateful she was that Tom had just texted her.

She began to think about her conversation with Lily at lunch and all of the emotions she had been through in the last four hours. Could it be that her interpretation of Tom, in general, was not accurate? She felt like there was a war going on among her emotions. The more attention she gave to it, the more she realized her emotions were getting the best of her.

She was not in charge of her emotions; her emotions were in charge of her.

This revelation was something that took her aback a bit. She certainly didn't want to feel victimized by herself! She looked over at the clock on the wall and it was almost two o'clock. Only a few more hours to go until I have the weekend, she thought.

She went over and she grabbed the pile of papers that she needed to work on, and once again sat down to attempt to get some work done. Maybe now that she had the text from Tom, she could concentrate.

The next two and a half hours dragged. Liz kept finding herself floating back and forth between work and personal thoughts. Ever since her conversation at lunch with Lily, she was painfully aware of how much that was happening. Up until this point she really had not given it much thought. It was just how her brain seemed to work. She had accepted this for years and it was the norm. She wondered if everyone else was this way. Did everyone else struggle as much as she did with thoughts showing up randomly?

Her tendency to get distracted was at a peak. Everything she did seemed like a futile attempt. Finally, after what felt like an eternity, she looked up at the clock and it was 4:30. It was the first time she moved quickly all day. Hurriedly, she collected all of the things that were around the office that she knew she would want for the weekend, straightened up her desk to make it look like she had actually accomplished something and set her voicemail for the weekend message.

Just as she finished, she received a text from Lily. 'I am ready when you are! Time to have some weekend fun!' it read.

Liz thought to herself, *I hope so,* and she snickered, looking at the smiling emoji.

The Ride Home - Day 2

The car was hot from the afternoon sun. Lily loved summer sunshine and all the heat that it brings. Liz immediately wanted the air conditioner on. She was not a fan of feeling hot. It often became a battle between the two of them as to whether or not to put the windows up or down or the air conditioning on or off. As soon as Liz reached for the air conditioning button, Lily laughed.

"I now realize how different we respond to things. I'm not going to get upset with you for turning the air conditioner on anymore," she said.

Liz had a dumbfounded look on her face. She didn't even realize this was something that had been on Lily's mind. Like a lightning bolt of awareness, Liz realized she was totally focused on herself. Her mind began to race as she thought about all the times she would reach over and turn the air conditioning on without ever asking Lily if she minded. She realized that many times she'd seen Lily put on a jacket or sweater and it never occurred to her that she might be making the environment uncomfortable.

Liz looked over at Lily and said, "I'm really sorry that I never thought about that before. Honestly, until you just said it, I hadn't realized I did that." Her head felt like it was spinning. How many times had she done this to other people and in different situations? Which other people in her life were experiencing similar feelings because she was completely unaware?

"It's really not that big of a deal. I know I'm often the cold one. People tell me all the time that the room is too warm when I am in it and they want to cool it off," Lily replied with a smirk.

The rest of the ride home, Liz was lost in her head. She was thinking about Tom and how she must do this to him at some points. She was thinking about how many times she had done this to Lily. She was thinking about how many times she had done this to other people and didn't even know. Basing all of her choices and decisions on herself and her own thoughts in the moment rather than paying attention to what was going on around her.

By the time they pulled into the driveway, Liz was convinced that she needed to work on this. She now was clear on the fact that it was not fair to be this unaware. She just had no idea where to begin and she was too tired to think about it right now.

She reached into the back seat, grabbed her bags and said to Lily, "I'm going to try to make tonight a better night somehow, I just don't know how."

Lily looked over her shoulder back at Liz and said, "Well, I'm here if you need me. Just text me and I'll be right over." With that, they parted ways for the evening.

Lily's Friday Night

As Lily walked in the door to her house, she noticed a large package on the counter in her kitchen. Immediately she got excited. A surprise! She rushed over to see if there was a note. On the side of the bag, there was a card that said *'Lily'* on the outside. She tore the card open and it said: "You're going to need these for tomorrow." A huge smile spread across Lily's face. Ben clearly had been planning their weekend. She could feel herself vibrating with joy and excitement.

Lily opened the package and inside was a new pair of hiking boots. A wave of uncertainty began to come over her. She knew that Ben loved to hike. However, she was not excited about hiking. Ever since she had met Ben, he was always trying to get her to go hiking. It wasn't that she didn't like going, it was just that sometimes the hikes were long, hot and tiring. He found such joy in hiking and she couldn't understand how. As she looked at the boots, she remembered the conversation that they had that morning. She told him she would be open to things that they could enjoy together, but this seemed to be something that he enjoyed and he was trying to get her to do it. A plethora of emotions were firing off in her head.

...And just like that, she remembered that she needed to ask who was driving her bus in this moment. *Who is driving my bus right this moment?* Lily asked herself. She felt as though it was anxiety and frustration, a mix of both really.

She picked the boots up and walked in and sat down and looked at them. "Okay, so I need to change this bus driver.

So I suppose I need to STOP, REFLECT, CHOOSE, and REDIRECT." Lily took a deep breath and went through the exercise of her mind. She decided that her new driver should be Curiosity. If she remained curious, she should be able to find out what Ben had in mind. If she chose to be frustrated or anxious, as she had been when she saw the boots, she would not be able to get anywhere. She would not be staying true to her word about letting him plan something without getting upset. "Okay! So curious it shall be," said Lily.

She went upstairs to put on her clothes to go out and do some gardening. As she walked up the stairs, she looked back at the dog and said, "I don't know what your daddy had in mind with these boots, but I sure hope he has a great idea."

When Ben came home, Lily was in the backyard. The moment she saw him, she wanted to start asking him about the boots and why hiking. Instead, she chose to get up and give him a hug and kiss. This was something that Ben did not expect. He knew she opened the package and he knew that she would be stressed out, but that was part of what he planned. Ben knew Lily better than anybody and he knew that she was going to be worried it would be an awful hiking trip again.

"Lily, I know you've seen the hiking boots because I see the package on the counter," Ben said.

Lily looked up from her flower bed and said, "Well, I must admit I did see them and I can't wait to hear what you have planned."

Ben looked dumbfounded. This was not what he expected at all. Lily rarely reacted like this and if this was the new version of their relationship, he was going to be excited.

"Well, I thought since you wanted to go and do that citywide gardening tour, hiking boots would be appropriate since it was such a long walk," Ben said.

Lily's face lit up like a delighted child. She quickly jumped to her feet and said, "Are you kidding me??? You really want to go and do that tour tomorrow? I didn't think that would be something that you would be interested in. I didn't even ask you because I know when I asked last year you thought that it would be boring and long."

Ben looked at her and smiled. "I did some research and it looks like there are lots of different things to see since it's through private homes. I'll probably be able to get some great ideas for projects that I want to build while you check out the gardens. I also figured we could go downtown and have a great brunch in the midst of it all, so I booked us a reservation at that French café you've wanted to try. Do you think that sounds like a fun weekend?"

Lily's eyes began to fill up with tears. "I think it sounds amazing and I'm glad I let you surprise me. I'm even happy you got me boots!" Lily gave Ben a huge hug. "So I guess that means tonight is a quiet night as we have so much walking to do tomorrow. How about if I just order some Chinese food, and I'll finish up out here in the yard and then we can get sleep before our long day tomorrow," said Lily.

"That sounds perfect," said Ben.

As Lily walked into the house to pick up the Chinese restaurant menu, she realized something new had just happened. She realized that all the anxiety and frustration with which she would have met this situation did not show up. She realized that having Curiosity remain the driver of her bus actually worked. By being curious, she did not react and by not reacting, her entire response to Ben was different. Because she had decided to be aware of her emotional state and then choose a better driver, she was going to have a day she had always wanted to have. Those gardening tours had been on her radar for years and they'd never been. Lily thought how amazing it was that by making a few small shifts, a lot had changed. If she stayed with Curiosity driving her bus, would she have even more interesting outcomes with Ben?

Over time, she had drifted away from the hobbies and activities that Ben liked. It wasn't that she wasn't interested in what Ben was doing, it was just that she was so focused on herself she didn't often think about his point of view, but with Curiosity driving, she could undoubtedly learn a lot about her husband.

That evening Ben and Lily had take-out Chinese food and laughed a lot. They watched a bad movie that they both agreed that they would never watch again. Lily didn't get stressed about chores that were not getting done. She actually didn't even care. They were going to have a great weekend. The chores should not be on her mind right now. What mattered was being able to spend time with someone she loved. After her talk with Liz about her and Tom, Lily realized how lucky she was and she was going to make sure that Ben knew that she felt like a lucky girl.

Liz's Evening

As Liz got into her house, she breathed a sigh of relief. Finally, she was in a place where no one had an expectation of her and she was alone. She clicked on the television in their living room and sat down on the couch. She thought to herself, *Maybe some brainless TV will help me chill out.* She began to flip through this seemingly endless number of channels they had and wondered, *Why do we have so many channels we don't watch?* Ironically, she settled on watching "I Love Lucy," something she loved when she was a child. *If Lucy can't make me happy, nobody can,* Liz thought. She was not sure how long it was going to be before Tom came home and she was not going to bother to check. She was completely exhausted. She knew that she was negative state of mind. As she sat on the couch watching Lucy and Ethel, she thought about Lily's story and the bus. She knew she had to change and she knew what was going on in her head was not helping her. It wasn't long before she drifted off to sleep with the TV still on and laughter in the background.

Liz woke up with Tom standing over her giving her a kiss on her forehead. "Hi Honey, I'm not sure if you're hungry, but I brought home some food. I tried texting you, but you weren't answering. I figured we'd try to get off to a good start after the last few days," said Tom.

Liz was groggy and hungry. She could smell the food and it didn't matter what he had in the bag. She was just hungry. "It's all good," said Liz. She walked into the kitchen and grabbed some plates out of the cabinet.

Tom followed her and they sat down at the kitchen table and began to empty the bag. Tom wasn't sure what to say because he didn't want to step on a landmine, causing Liz to blow up at him. Liz was too tired to talk. She just wanted things to be better, but she didn't know how to do that. She kept thinking about how to change things and how to change Tom. She felt like she was on a go-cart track in her head. Always circling and circling but getting nowhere.

Tom got up from the table to put some music on and immediately, Liz said to him, "It's too loud, please turn it down." As he walked back into the kitchen, Liz realized that she said that in a very rude way. "Awareness is the foundation of everything," said the voice in her head, something Lily had said this very afternoon. *Right,* Liz thought to herself. "I'm sorry, Tom, I didn't mean to bark at you like that. I just have so much in my head right now and I don't want to take it out on you. The music is fine," said Liz. Tom just looked at her and smiled.

The rest of the evening at Liz and Tom's house was quiet.

Tom was surprised that Liz didn't want to talk about anything, nor did she try to wear him down; instead, she didn't speak. They sat on opposite ends of the couch and watched a movie. Liz struggled to keep track of what was going on in her head. She went from one emotion to the other. By the end of the movie, Liz was completely exhausted. She looked over at Tom and said, "I'm just going to go to bed now. I can't believe how tired I am and I think if I have a good night sleep I might feel better about everything tomorrow."

As she began to walk away, Tom reluctantly reminded her that he was going golfing tomorrow with two of his friends from work. Tom knew that Liz hated it when he went golfing on Saturdays. He knew that she would want him to do things with her on Saturday. Even though he had told her about this a couple of weeks ago, she made a face. As Liz heard the words come out of Tom's mouth, she felt frustration bubbling up.

"Okay, well I guess then I'll have to take care of everything by myself, yet again," Liz said.

Tom came back sharply, "I never said I wouldn't do the things you wanted me to do. I just said I was going golfing. When do I not do the things you ask me to do? No matter what you ask me to do, it gets done. It just may not get done the moment you want it done or how you want it done. But I do get it done.

You're not the only one who has stress Liz and when I get to go out and golf, it makes me happy. I am sorry you're pissed off at me, but I told you about this and I'm going to go. Leave me a list of the chores that you want to be done and I will get them done."

Liz walked up the stairs and into the bedroom. As she shut the bedroom door, she began to cry. Why did it all have to be so hard? Why did it seem endlessly challenging to do this thing called marriage? She crawled into bed and fell asleep with all of the emotions unresolved and very heavy thoughts running through her mind.

Saturday - Day Three of the Challenge

Lily's Saturday

Saturday morning began early for Lily. She woke up before the alarm sounded. As she laid there waking up, she began to think of how grateful she was.

Thoughts of love and appreciation washed through her mind. The simplest of things in Lily's life started to become places for her to find gratitude. So many times in her life, Lily had just jumped out of bed and had never given a thought to being grateful before her day began. This process of pausing and putting Gratitude in the driver's seat of her bus immediately was changing the way she thought.

By the time she got out of bed, she felt like the luckiest girl in the world, and besides, it was Saturday and she was about to have an epic day of garden touring! She ran downstairs to let the dog out and make the coffee. She thought to herself, *It's early enough for me to run to the bakery and get us some fresh pastries for breakfast!*

As soon as the dog was back in the house, she put on his collar, grabbed his leash and asked him if he wanted to go for a ride. Off to the bakery they went. The entire drive to the bakery, Lily was focused on choosing to be Excited. She kept finding her bus being hijacked by Certainty and the need to know that she would get to see everything through the gardening tour. This was a trait that showed up often for Lily.

She had to always be first at every event. Even leaving to go on vacation, she had to be at the airport extremely early because she wanted to be at the gate of the plane first. She never wanted to miss anything or feel that she had left somewhere without seeing everything. Many times this had caused her and Ben to argue.

Ben felt the most crucial part of all of their adventures was just to enjoy being together. Ben lived more in the moment than Lily did. So today, remembering all of this, Lily was making it a point to be in a state of Excitement and just enjoy each piece of it, whatever they got to see. By the time she got back from the bakery, she had devised a plan.

Lily grabbed the brochure from the day's event and began to look at the map. Typically she would want to see every house that was open for the garden tour. Today she decided to only highlight the ones that were "must-see gardens" so that she knew her top five houses were covered. The rest would be a bonus.

She knew that it would surprise Ben and she was proud of herself for thinking of it. Life was changing little by little. She was proud of herself for allowing the changes to take place instead of focusing on missing things and letting Anxiety drive her bus. She was focused on Curiosity, Excitement and seeing the top five houses.

When Ben came down the stairs and saw his favorite pastry and coffee ready, along with Lily smiling and telling him the story of the map and what she had decided to do, he couldn't have been more excited. "Lily, I don't know what's going on or how you're pulling this off, but I am incredibly proud of you. I feel like I am married to a new woman. Not that I want to be married to a new woman, but I certainly feel like you are different than you have been," said Ben.

Lily smiled from ear to ear and gave Ben a big hug. "Thank you for noticing and thank you for being patient with me. I'm telling you that I am committed to changing after learning about who is driving my bus, I can't go back to just letting my emotions rule me. I am going to rule my emotions as much as I can. If I can do this at least 80% of the time, I know my life will improve and our lives will change for the better," said Lily.

Lily and Ben finished eating breakfast. They talked about what Lily wanted to make sure to see. So they laid out their plan for the day. Ben suggested to Lily to shower and he would run the dog through the neighborhood while she got ready. This would save time and they could get there early.

Lily felt like a million dollars at that moment. She felt like Ben understood her and her needs. Even though Certainty was not driving her bus, she still liked it.

She wondered if she'd ever stop having a need to be the first one in line. Though the truth is it didn't really matter. As long as she was not emotionally attached to being first, she could be first every single time. Her emotional reaction to being first was the problem, not the simple act of *being* first. She could still work hard at being on time and being the first one in line as long as she didn't get Angry, Frustrated, or Anxious driving her bus in the process.

By the time Ben came back with the dog, Lily was almost ready. She was packing up her camera and her backpack with snacks and water. Ben jumped in the shower and within 15 minutes, they were in the car on the way to the first house. Lily was confident they would be among the first to arrive and she was very excited about that. While they were driving, Lily looked down at her new hiking boots and thought, "How appropriate for me to be walking in new shoes with my brand new bus driver."

The first part of their day went by quickly. They were able to see four of Lily's top five houses before brunch and that was without rushing. Lily was so excited because of all the photos she took and everything she was learning. Ben found some really great ideas for how to restructure their vegetable gardens and trellises. By the time they went to have brunch, they couldn't wait to share ideas about what they wanted to do with their yard.

Brunch was wonderful in the courtyard filled with blooming wisteria. The fragrance was intoxicating and both Ben and Lily were inspired to create a spot in their backyard where they could grow wisteria over their porch. At one point, Lily felt her eyes fill up with happy tears. She looked over at Ben and said, "I am so grateful for this day that we are having. You really are my best friend and I don't tell you that enough. Thank you for loving me." Ben leaned over and kissed her and said: "I love you and I love that we are growing together." Being able to be this relaxed was new for Lily. She really loved how effortless this day felt. She completely and totally recognized that understanding her bus driver was changing her. She understood what an unresourceful bus driver she had most of the time and while there were times that Certainty was undoubtedly the best bus driver, having her be the default driver was really not a great idea.

Just then the waitress came and put their check down, so off they went, time to get back on the tour.

By the end of the day, they toured ten houses! Lily was shocked that they made it through as many as they did, given the size of the properties and what they had to offer. On the way home, Lily looked at the houses they had missed on the map and realized that there was no way in one day anyone could possibly cover that many houses and actually enjoy each house. To get through all the houses that were open for viewing, guests would have to do it so quickly that they wouldn't be able to appreciate each one.

She began to think about how many times in her life she had rushed through things just to be able to say she went through them. This was something that she was going to make it a point to work on. She knew there was work in this area to do and she was going to pay attention to putting Patient Girl in the driver's seat of her bus every chance she could.

Lily and Ben were exhausted by the end of the day. They went home and took the dog for a leisurely walk around the pond. They talked about all the cool things they had seen and what they wanted to do in their backyard. Lily could not remember the last time they had such a special day together. She was going to make sure this would not be a rare occasion. She realized how much control she actually did have by showing up differently within her marriage. She knew that it would take both of them to be different; however, she knew that by her choosing to be different, it could change everything.

Liz's Saturday

The sunshine was streaming across the wall above Liz's head. She was groggy and had no idea what time it was. She felt like her body weighed a thousand pounds. It was late morning, much later than Liz ever slept, and she had no idea why she felt so strange. As she began to wake up, she realized the dog was lying across her legs. Maybe that was why she felt so heavy, or perhaps it was because she slept too long. As her senses began to come back to her, she remembered her argument with Tom. Within a moment, her mind was filled with emotions. She was Exhausted, Frustrated, Angry, Sad, and most of all, Overwhelmed.

She began to replay the events of the last 48 hours in her head, like watching a bad movie over and over even though you know you don't like the ending. As she laid there in her bed, tears began to run down her cheeks. The funny thing was that nothing had actually happened at this moment. Liz was crying simply because she was running the thoughts of the last 48 hours in her head. Not because anything new had happened. Liz, however, did not realize this.

Liz was being run by her emotions. She was clearly not in charge of them; they were in charge of her. All she could think about was how Tom didn't care about her. As she got out of bed and worked her way into the bathroom, she was expanding on her story about how little he must care for her. She began to paint pictures in her mind of how dreadful their relationship was and how unimportant she was to him. Unfortunately, Liz was stuck in a loop. By the time she put her clothes on to take the dog for a walk and go downstairs, the tears were streaming fully down her face.

As she walked around her kitchen to make her coffee, she looked for any sign that Tom was still home. She then remembered that he was golfing and another flood of desperation and anger seared through her mind. "How could he just leave and go golfing knowing that we have such problems?" Liz said out loud. She began a rant that lasted the entire time she was making coffee. By the time she was ready to go out the door with the dog, she had worked herself up to being extremely angry. She grabbed her phone and texted Tom... "What time will you be back?"

The funny thing was that she knew texting him was pointless since Tom always left his phone in the truck when he played golf. Asking him a question like this was not going to get an answer. Liz decided to take the long trail around the pond with the dog. Maybe a walk would calm her down. As they ventured off, she barely noticed all the beautiful things around her. Flowers were blooming everywhere. The sun was shining bright and the air was refreshing. She didn't notice the ducks in the pond. She didn't really hear the birds singing either. Liz was in another world; an inner world that she had created for herself, and was in complete control over, and it was one that made her miserable. She walked the dog for over an hour, much longer than usual. Even when the dog tried to get her to play, she didn't seem to notice him. By the time they got back to the house, it was lunchtime. Liz had slept in so late that the whole first part of the day was gone. As she walked into her kitchen and sat down at the counter, she began to think about all the chores she had to do. "How much more could this suck. It's a beautiful day and I have chores to do." Liz said, talking out loud to herself. She completely missed the fact that she had already been enjoying the beautiful day outside but didn't take a moment to reflect to recognize that and enjoy it in the process. Instead, she was focused on the notion that she was missing something.

So she dove into her chores, miserable and resentful. It never occurred to her that it didn't have to be this way. She was entrenched in her story and she was sticking with it.

The rest of the afternoon seemed like a blur. Liz did laundry, vacuuming and gave the dog a bath. She ran out to the grocery store and got supplies. She paid bills. By the time she finished, she had worked herself to such a state that she felt sick to her stomach. She skipped eating lunch and that only made things worse. It was late in the afternoon now and she knew that Tom would be finished golfing anytime. She could not wait for him to get home so that she could have a conversation with him about all of this. She wanted to be prepared so she went upstairs and she decided to take a shower. The entire time she was in the shower she was focused on everything she would tell him. All of the offenses she could think of were streaming through her mind like a marching band playing their tune of dissatisfaction. Once again, she was not paying attention to the things around her that were wonderful. She had a brand-new master bathroom that was beautiful and her shower was luxurious. The rainfall shower-head that Tom installed specially for her went unnoticed. At no point did the emotion of dissatisfaction consider that Tom had designed the master suite specifically for her.

As Liz was drying her hair, she thought about how unhappy she was with herself. She looked in the mirror and she thought she looked old and drawn out. She commented to herself about how her eyes had dark circles. She believed she looked terrible. She thought that must be the reason why Tom was disinterested in her. Her level of Judgement soared. She completely forgot how hard she had been working on her body. She completely forgot about how often Tom mentioned that she looked great. She was drifting down a dark road in her mind of Judgement and Despair.

It was getting close to the time Tom would show up from playing golf. Her mind was spinning with all the things that she thought she would say to Tom. The more she thought about it, the more aggravated she became. Much like a windup toy, she was entering into a spin. When she realized that Tom had never texted her back about what time he would be back, she had a flicker of Fear jolt her. "What if he decides to not come home?" she said to the dog. From that moment until the time that Tom walked in the door, she went back and forth between Fear and Anger. The entire time this happened, she was unconscious of what was happening. It was clear she was not thinking about the conversation that she had with Lily about controlling emotions. She was not driving her emotions, her emotions were driving her.

She heard the screen door shut at the back of the house and she knew Tom was home. As he walked around the corner into the kitchen, she was ready to let him have it. As she turned the corner in anger, she saw him standing in the kitchen with a big bouquet of flowers in his hand and a smile on his face.

All of her emotions began to flood through her at once and she began to cry. "Why are you crying?" Tom asked.

"I honestly have no idea. I'm a complete train wreck and I know it. I have no idea why I'm so frustrated and nasty sometimes because I do love you, I'm just not sure if I like myself right now," said Liz.

"Here's what I know, Liz, I love you and I'm not leaving you. I don't like the way we fight and I don't like the fact that I feel uncomfortable in my own house. But what I do like is that when we're good, we're really great. I know I need to do a better job of helping around the house. It would help me immensely if you could just do a better job at not seeing everything that I do as wrong. It never makes anyone feel good when they feel like everything they do is wrong. I know you don't mean it, but it pushes me away. I do want to fix it though and I am willing to work at it," said Tom.

Liz sat there on the bar stool in the kitchen, just listening. She had known for quite some time that she was running on empty and she hadn't been doing anything to fix it. She knew that they could not continue on like this. "I know... I know. I've known for a long time; it's not all your fault. I just don't know how to fix anything within myself. Thank you for coming home with flowers. It means a lot to me," said Liz. She got up and went to the sink with the flowers to put them in water. Liz began thinking about all the time she had wasted today. She couldn't help thinking that her entire Saturday had been spent being an emotional disaster. She bent over and smelt the flowers and thought to herself, *'Flowers seem to make everything better.'*

That evening Liz and Tom didn't talk very much. They decided to get some takeout and just hang out and watch a movie. It felt good to sit and just 'be' with Tom instead of trying to figure anything out. Liz thought about how proud Lily would be of her for just relaxing. Suddenly, as if a lightning bolt had come into her brain, she thought about her conversation with Lily and the 72-hour challenge. She grabbed her phone and texted Lily *'Can you please send me over the links to the 72-hour challenge that you were talking about today? The link for the book? All of it... I need to change things for myself and I need to do it quickly'.*

She looked over at Tom and she said, "I'm going to try this challenge that Lily and Ben are doing and if it works for me then you can do it too if you're interested. Lily told me all about it this week at work. I have to admit that I'm skeptical, at least I was skeptical, but I realize now I've got to do something and I need to do something quickly. So I just asked her to send me over all the information," said Liz.

Tom smiled and said, "Whatever we need to do, just tell me and we'll do it."

Almost immediately, Liz's phone buzzed. 'Here's everything you need! I'm really excited for you and I'm really excited for all of us. I just had the most amazing Saturday with Ben. I feel like I'm more in love with him than ever and quite honestly nothing has changed BUT ME! Sure he's changing a little, well maybe a lot, I'm not really sure. The one thing I know is that I'm not focused on what he's doing. I am focusing on what I'm doing and that's making all the difference,' texted Lily.

Liz took a deep breath. She knew that this would not be easy for her. But she knew something had to change. And with that, she went upstairs and grabbed her tablet.

Life was about to change for the better...

THE 72 Hour Challenge

Whether you have just finished reading the book or you have just jumped to this section before you started the book, the 72 Hour Challenge is a major component to achieving success in managing your emotions.

Becoming aware of what is going on in your head, how your emotions are affecting you and how often this happens is the foundation to change.

If you would like to watch the video, please go to authorkimjohnson.com/72hourchallenge for an in-depth explanation.

If you would like to dive in, the steps are as follows:

1. Ask yourself if you are honestly committed to the ENTIRE 72 hours of the challenge. It takes the commitment of being "all in" in order not to quit when it gets tough and you become frustrated.

2. Decide how you will record your tracking. I am a big fan of thought capturing in a small note book. However a notes app or texting yourself are also strategies that my clients utilize.

3. Before the 72 hours begin, sit down and write out all the emotions you believe you experience during the day. Really think about your day, your week and remember how your emotions transitioned.

4. Write out any situations and/or people that push your buttons and that trigger your emotions.

5. Set your 72 hour start time. It's best to begin when you get out bed. Immediately notice which emotion you are experiencing while waking up.

6. From the moment you wake up till the moment you go to sleep, every time that you are aware of the emotion you are in, record it. Be aware that emotions change rapidly and often. This is the very reason that this exercise require patience with yourself. While it is a simple exercise, it is certainly not easy!

7. You will most likely notice that you stay within a small selection of emotions, looping through 3 - 5 different ones. This is very normal.

8. As you become aware of your emotions, you will begin to find them shifting by the very act of identifying them.

9. During this challenge, stay consistent with identifying as many as you can. The point is to find out how much time you stay in particular emotions and how much that emotion restricts your progress.

10. Ask yourself if the emotion you are experiencing is serving you. By recognizing whether or not the emotion is serving you, you can begin to see the reason this exercise is so helpful.

11. Laugh at yourself. Find humor in the way your mind and emotions are working. It's inevitable that you will judge yourself for how you feel. Again, that's perfectly fine. It's all very normal.

12. Keep up the recording for the entire 72 hours so you have a solid record of where your emotions go. Give yourself the gift of knowing what goes on in your head.

If you have already read the book, you can layer the 72 hours like Lily in the story, identify and shifting your emotions. Whether you decide to just identify your emotions in the first 72 hours or identify and shift your emotions as Lily did, you will come to a new level of awareness.

Remember, this should be fun! Don't be so hard on yourself and again, be patient. You've got this!

Gratitude Driving Your Bus

Clients often ask me, “Who is the best driver for my bus?”

The truth is that there is not a “best driver.” There is only the best driver for each situation and moment. However, I personally have found that in the moments of my day when I am not utilizing specific drivers that I choose, Gratitude is my go-to girl. Sure, my Hippie Chick Zen Girl is incredible at getting me calmed down and centered again, but Gratitude Girl allows me to see details of my life that I would definitely be missing without her.

Gratitude, in my humble opinion and observation, is the most powerful of all the emotions available to us. It is a direct derivative of Love, giving us the gift of Awe.

Our world is abundant with wonder. Most of us are completely missing it. We have become creatures attached to electronic leashes responding to every ping we hear on our phones. We give up human interaction for our electronic addiction. We miss the incredible, small gifts all around us.

When you begin to cultivate Gratitude, like you would cultivate a garden, you yield abundance.

Many of us have heard of the concept of a morning & evening gratitude list. The challenge with that practice is that it leaves you open to being ‘checked out' the moment you put your list down, until the moment you pick your list up again. The list is a good beginning; however, it will not transform you rapidly. When you practice with the power of gratitude, working this emotion like a magic wand, your perspective of the world expands exponentially.

Gratitude is a power that most of us only have fleeting interaction with, never really resonating in the glory of the full emotion for an extended period of time. When you cultivate your skill for choosing Gratitude, you have begun to understand the magic it possesses.

Choose Gratitude as a bus driver as often and as long as you can. Allow yourself to find new things to be grateful for instead of the 'standard list' we seem to have as our go-to. Make this adventure a treasure hunt, seeking and finding new curiosities. Use all of your senses to experience your world and find new things to be grateful for every day, every moment. In the beginning, allow your senses to identify things for you. For instance, my sense of vision can be Grateful for anything it sees, even a paper clip as silly as that sounds. Honestly, though, I have been Grateful for a paper clip with its astonishingly simple design and yet so effective performance!

Don't wait for someone to deliver magic to you. Make your own magic using Gratitude.

As I sit here, finishing this book, I am grateful for the music playing, the gentle breeze, the warm weather, the perfect height of this picnic table at which I'm sitting, the fact that my son is skating in a fabulous skate park, the gorgeous sunset happening, the new friends he is making, the jacket that I packed in my bag (I am always chilly), the other boys that are helping him learn so much about skateboarding, my mac, the fingers that are typing this, the Creativity that loves writing and making art of any kind...do you see? This was just my surface scan...a blip in time, an observational moment. I could go on and on.

And with that, I am extremely grateful you joined Lily, Liz and me on this journey. My hope is that you have found some pearls of wisdom that will help you shift your world for the better and allow you to control Who Is Driving Your Bus. Enjoy your trip, my friends!

Namaste,

Kim

Absorbed
Abhorrence
Acceptance
Admiration
Adoration
Adrift
Aching
Affection
Afraid
Agitated
Agony
Aggravated
Alarm
Alert
Alienated
Alive
Alone
Amazed
Amused
Anger
Angst
Animated
Animosity
Animus
Annoyed
Antagonistic
Anticipation
Antipathy
Antsy
Anxiety
Apathetic
Apologetic
Appalled
Appreciative
Apprehensive
Ardor
Arousal
Astonishment
Astounded
Attachment
Attraction
Aversion
Awe
Awkward
Baffled

Bashful
Befuddled
Bemused
Betrayed
Bewildered
Bitter
Blessed
Bliss
Blithe
Blue
Bold
Bonhomie
Boredom
Bothered
Bouncy
Brave
Breathless
Brooding
Bubbly
Buoyant
Burning
Calm
Captivated
Carefree
Caring
Cautious
Certain
Chagrin
Challenged
Chary
Cheerful
Choked
Choleric
Clueless
Cocky
Cold
Collected
Comfortable
Commiseration
Committed
Compassionate
Complacent
Complaisance
Composed
Compunction

Confused
Courage
Concerned
Confident
Conflicted
Consternation
Contemplative
Contempt
Contentment
Contrition
Cordial
Cowardly
Crafty
Cranky
Craving
Crestfallen
Cross
Cruel
Crummy
Crushed
Curious
Cynical
Defeated
Dejection
Delectation
Delighted
Delirious
Denial
Derisive
Desire
Desolation
Despair
Despondent
Detached
Determined
Detestation
Devastated
Devotion
Disappointed
Disbelief
Disdain
Disgruntled
Disgust
Disillusioned
Disinterested

Dismay
Distaste
Distracted
Distress
Disturbed
Doleful
Dopey
Doubtful
Down
Downcast
Drained
Dread
Dubious
Dumbfounded
Eager
Earnest
Ease
Ebullient
Ecstatic
Edgy
Elated
Embarrassment
Empathic
Empty
Enchantment
Energetic
Engrossed
Enjoyment
Enlightenment
Enmity
Entertainment
Enthralled
Enthusiasm
Envy
Euphoria
Exasperated
Excitement
Excluded
Exhausted
Exhilaration
Expectant
Exuberant
Fanatical
Fascinated
Fatigued

Feisty
Felicitous
Fervor
Flabbergasted
Floored
Fondness
Foolish
Foreboding
Fortunate
Frazzled
Free
Fretful
Frightened
Frustrated
Fulfilled
Furious
Genial
Giddy
Glad
Gleeful
Gloomy
Goofy
Gratified
Grateful
Greedy
Grief
Groggy
Grudging
Guarded
Guilt
Gung-ho
Gusto
Hankering
Happy
Harassed
Hatred
Heartache
Heartbroken
Helpless
Hesitant
Hollow
Homesick
Hopeful
Horrified
Hostile

Humiliated
Humored
Hurt
Hyper
Hysterical
Impatient
Incensed
Indifferent
Indignant
Infatuated
Inferior
Inspired
Intense
Interested
Intimacy
Intimidated
Intoxicated
Intrigued
Introspective
Invigorated
Irascible
Ire
Irritated
Isolated
Jaded
Jealous
Jittery
Jocular
Jocund
Jolly
Jovial
Joy
Jubilant
Jumpy
Keen
Lazy
Left out
Lethargic
Liberation
Lighthearted
Liking
Listless
Lively
Lonely
Longing

Lost
Love
Lucky
Lust
Mad
Meditative
Melancholic
Mellow
Merry
Miffed
Mirth
Mischievous
Miserable
Mollified
Mortified
Motivated
Mournful
Moved
Mystified
Nasty
Nauseous
Needy
Nervous
Neutral
Nonplussed
Nostalgic
Numb
Obsessed
Offended
Optimistic
Outrage
Overwhelmed
Pacified
Pain
Panic
Paranoid
Passion
Pathetic
Peaceful
Peevish
Pensive
Perky
Perplexed
Perturbed
Pessimistic
Petrified
Petty
Petulant
Phlegmatic
Pity
Playful
Pleasure
Positive
Possessive
Powerful
Powerless
Preoccupied
Protective
Proud
Psyched
Pumped
Puzzled
Quizzical
Rage
Rapture
Rattled
Reassured
Receptive
Reflective
Regret
Relaxed
Relief
Relish
Reluctance
Remorse
Repugnance
Resentment
Resignation
Restless
Revolted
Sad
Sanguine
Satisfied
Scandalized
Scorn
Secure
Self-Conscious
Selfish
Sensual
Sensitive
Serendipitous
Serene
Settled
Shaken
Shame
Sheepish
Shock
Shy
Sick
Silly
Sincere
Skeptical
Sluggish
Smug
Snappy
Solemn
Solicitous
Somber
Sore
Sorrow
Sorry
Sour
Speechless
Spiteful
Sprightly
Stirred
Stressed
Strong
Stung
Stunned
Stupefied
Submissive
Succor
Suffering
Suffocated
Sullen
Sunny
Superior
Sure
Surprised
Startled
Sympathy
Tenderness
Tense
Terror

Testy
Tetchy
Thankful
Thirst
Thoughtful
Thrill
Timid
Tired
Titillation
Tormented
Torn
Torture
Touched
Traumatized
Tranquil
Trepidation
Triumphant
Troubled
Trust
Twitchy
Upbeat
Upset
Uptight
Vehement
Vexation
Vigilant
Vindication
Vindictive
Warmth
Wary
Weak
Weary
Welcome
Woe
Wonder
Woozy
Worry
Wrath
Wretched
Yearning
Zeal
Zest

Kim has been professionally involved in the self-development industry since 1996, studying with and working for, the best-known professionals in the industry. She has over 20,000 hours in coaching clients and holds certifications in NLP, Cognitive Behavioral Therapy, and is a Certified Master Practitioner Coach.

Even though she has had the good fortune to coach thousands of people, Kim still considers the daily work she does on herself to be the most challenging.

One of her core tenets is to always have the internal fortitude and grit to do the level of work within herself that she expects from her clients. Because of this, she stuck to her creative dreams and is the proud author of multiple books, including: *Nail It In 90, Nail It In 90 for Direct Selling & Network Marketing, The Things In Your Head, Who Would You Be, Today I Decided* and *The Adventures of Shelley Crabster and the New Pink Shell.*

Kim enjoys her life living in South Carolina with her husband, two children, two dogs, one cat, one mouse and twelve snakes.

Other books by Kim Johnson are all available on Amazon.

www.authorkimjohnson.com

Made in the USA
Monee, IL
06 April 2024